Training the Hard to Train Dog

tfh

Peggy Swager

Training the Hard-to-Train Dog

Project Team
Editor: Heather Russell-Revesz
Copy Editor: Stephanie Fornino
Indexer: Lucie Haskins
Design: Mary Ann Kahn

TFH Publications
President/CEO: Glen S. Axelrod
Executive Vice President: Mark E. Johnson
Publisher: Christopher T. Reggio
Production Manager: Kathy Bontz

TFH Publications, Inc.
One TFH Plaza
Third and Union Avenues
Neptune City, NJ 07753

Printed and bound in China
11 12 13 14 15   5 7 9 8 6

Library of Congress Cataloging-in-Publication Data
Swager, Peggy O.
  Training the hard-to-train dog : effective training techniques for working with shy, controlling, and stubborn dogs / Peggy Swager.
    p. cm.
  ISBN 978-0-7938-0667-6 (alk. paper)
  1. Dogs--Training. 2. Dogs--Behavior. 3. Dog breeds. I. Title.
  SF431.S93 2008
  636.7'0835--dc22
                              2008024055

The Leader In Responsible Animal Care For Over 50 Years!®
www.tfh.com

Table of Contents

Introduction

Several dogs led to my development as a trainer. While growing up, the most memorable dog my family owned was a Golden Retriever cross named Brutus. Although I didn't realize it at the time, Brutus was relatively easy to train. In fact, he was one of the best-trained dogs I've ever owned. Over the years, I'd trained all my dogs with little difficulty—until Cookie, my next notable dog. The harsh "smack-the-dog-when-he's-bad" techniques (still used at the time) didn't work with this Jack Russell Terrier, so I

spent years studying and learning new dog-training techniques. These included clicker training and reward-based techniques, as well as learning from several professional trainers whose experience ranged from training bomb-sniffing dogs to showing in obedience.

Cookie's stubbornness forced me to learn how to train a dog with that kind of a nature, and I began my education with renowned mule trainer Brad Cameron.

Attempting to teach Cookie agility also forced me to further my education on techniques for training a dog to comply when there is no natural motivation for him to do so. (Cookie had so little interest in doing agility that she would sometimes wander out of the show ring.)

For many years, I taught dog-training classes and did private consulting for problem dogs. In 2002, my article on overly submissive behavior won a Dog Writers Association of America (DWAA) award for best training article. However, my greatest challenge in working with dogs with a more sensitive nature lay ahead.

I decided to acquire a dog who wouldn't have Cookie's many quirky characteristics (like

Brutus, a Golden Retriever Mix (previous page), and Cookie, a Jack Russell Terrier (right), helped with my development as a dog trainer.

so many Jack Russell Terriers have) that can make them an overwhelming training challenge. Remembering how great Brutus was, I purchased a Golden Retriever– Australian Shepherd mix named Aspen. As it turned out, Aspen was far from easy to train. She was what I call an "over-the-top dog" with excess energy, a high drive, an overly sensitive nature, and a tendency for dominance. Around the time Aspen came into my life, I began working with a Jack Russell Terrier named Lestat, a dog I later came to own. He also offered a lot of challenges. He ran the gambit from very pushy and defiant social climber to overly sensitive when told "no." Dealing with such challenging traits all wrapped up in one dog demanded that I highly refine my training skills. In all honesty, had I not owned Cookie, Aspen, and Lestat, this book would not be possible.

People have trained dogs for years. Some old-school techniques, where choke chains are used to dominate the dog and punishment employed to deter unwanted behaviors, are not good for the dog but will manage to get the job done with a more tolerant canine. However, I have learned the hard way that when these harsh techniques are used on dogs with more problematic characteristics, behavior disasters can occur. Even when using "good" techniques, which strive to teach the dog what you want rather than punish what you don't want, I've found that there is no one technique that works for the same problem behavior in all personalities of dogs. For this reason, this book not only discusses breed traits that make some dogs more challenging to train, but it also offers a variety of techniques to help find the most effective way to resolve behavior issues.

GettingStarted

PartOne

Chapter One

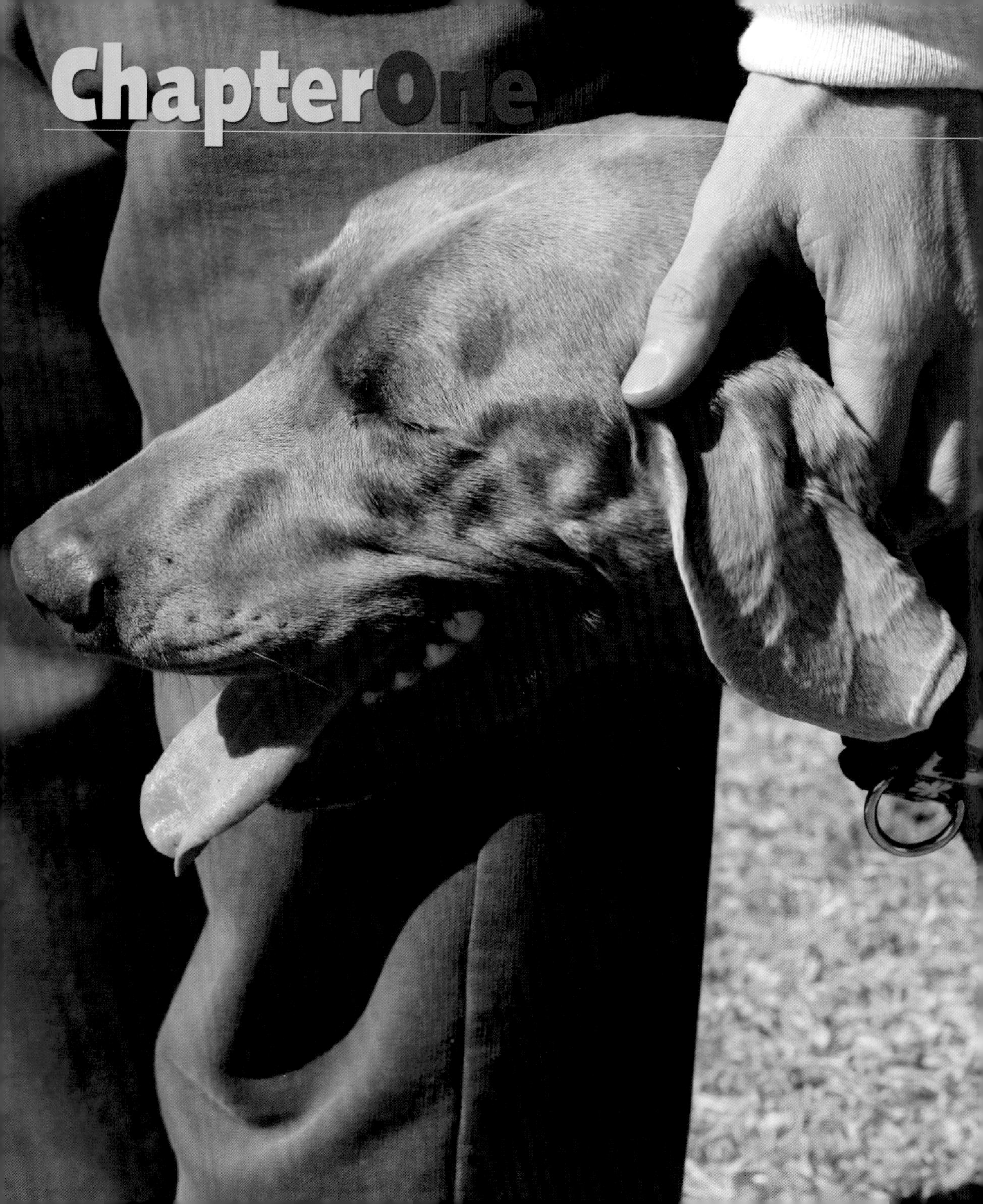

The Importance of Becoming Your Dog's Leader

Before you learn how to train your hard-to-train dog, it's important to understand something about dog behavior. You can find many behavior books that go into detail about packs, pack hierarchy, and dog interactions. What I'd like to touch on in this chapter is how certain traits related to pack order and dominance affect training and your relationship with your dog.

Dogs and Wolves

For years, dog trainers correlated behavior information from the study of wolves to that of dogs. Now, that concept has fallen out of vogue. While there are indeed some traits and behaviors that dogs and wolves share, the dog has changed after years of domestication. Even similar behaviors, such as marking, do not have the same significance for dogs and wolves. Darleen Kobobel, founder and president of Colorado Wolf and Wildlife Center, has worked with both wolves and dogs for years, and she helped introduce me to a new perspective on the similarities and differences between them.

Wolf Pack Structure

As far as pack structure is concerned, wolves have alpha males and beta females as leaders. The alpha makes the rules for the pack and controls the resources and privileges. Those resources and privileges are important to the wolves' survival and dictate who gets to eat first, where the animal sleeps, and even breeding privileges. The alpha male and female are the only two wolves in the pack who are allowed to breed, which is not true for dogs. The alpha has what can be viewed as a power aura—a certain presence, immediately acknowledged by the other wolves, communicated with body postures and the way in which the wolf carries and conducts himself. Both the alpha male and the beta female will mark territory and then scratch afterward, which also marks territory because of the scent glands in between

While there are some traits and behaviors that dogs and wolves share, after years of domestication, the dog has changed.

their toes. Dog marking doesn't seem to have quite the same significance that wolf marking does.

The alpha wolf uses the tools nature gave him to enforce his power and maintain his status. Some of those tools include alpha rolls (posturing over other wolves and often standing rigid and growling) and sometimes even biting the subordinate.

According to Darlene, as far as pack structure is concerned, all the other wolves in the pack fall in an order of hierarchy and do not have the privileges of the two leaders. The top wolf is the alpha. His second in command is the beta, the female. At the bottom of the pack are the omegas, who are shy, walk around with their tails between their legs, and are quick to offer submissive behaviors, which include peeing and exposing their belly when around wolves of higher status. Omega wolves seem to always stay at the bottom of the pack. After puppies are born, an omega may sometimes change his (or her) status when he realizes that there are individuals lower than him. However, an omega wolf will never move that far in the hierarchy. Some dogs show similar behaviors as omega wolves when it comes to submissive behaviors, including rolling on their back to expose their belly to show their submission.

Domesticated Wolves?

According to Darlene, attempts have been made to further the domestication of wolves by taking a two-week-old wolf pup and working extensively to socialize the animal. The pup was kept with a human 24 hours a day, 7 days a week. The result? Wolf traits still dominate the animal's behavior. Wolves raised in this manner won't respond to humans the same way that dogs will. Dogs can be trained and live harmoniously with humans because generations of selective breeding have created different

Wolf Dogs

Some people like the idea of having what is often called a wolf hybrid, or more accurately, a wolf dog. (A true hybrid can't reproduce; wolf dogs can.) Darlene Kobobel, founder and president of Colorado Wolf and Wildlife Center, has seen a variety of wolf characteristics displayed in these crosses (wolf with a dog and wolf dog to wolf dog), making them impossible to keep as pets.

The Colorado Wolf and Wildlife Center is full, but unfortunately, Darlene still gets calls to take on wolves or wolf dogs as frequently as once per day. Humane societies can't place wolf dogs, so they are immediately destroyed. More information about these kinds of animals can be found on Colorado Wolf and Wildlife Center's website at www.wolfeducation.org.

characteristics that allow it. While wolves can be trained to a certain extent, that trainability is no different than training any wild animal—it doesn't compare to the trainability of a dog. Unlike dogs, wolves don't want to be your companion, and they don't have the same motivation to please. Also, a wolf will not view you as the leader, while a dog will—you can never be part of a wolf pack in a wolf's eyes.

Is the Alpha Dog a Myth?

Great controversy has arisen in recent years about the concept of an alpha dog. Some dog behaviorists feel that this perception of dog behavior is not warranted—that there is no such thing

Too Easy?

An easy-to-train dog who follows even poor leadership can lead to trouble. Owners often end up with a fairly compliant dog, even if they use few or poor training techniques. Then, when they get a new dog who doesn't behave well under the same conditions, they blame the dog. The truth of the matter is that the owner needs to learn better training techniques and good leadership skills, both of which will lead to a much happier dog and a better relationship with him.

as an alpha dog. In my experience, I have seen dogs who take on a natural leadership role—dogs who have a presence that other dogs seem to sense and will often yield to. This type of dog is allowed first access to resources by the other dogs. However, keep in mind that the structure seen in a wolf pack is diluted in dog culture and that dogs do fit into our pack, while wolves do not. The problem with alpha dogs, I think, is not whether dogs can be "alpha" but whether behavior issues can or should be blamed on "alpha-ness." When people equate unwanted behavior with a dog being an alpha, it's usually just an excuse to use bullying training methods—and bullying a dog is not a good technique. If, on the off chance, you do indeed own an actual alpha dog, you can manage him without using a harsh voice, alpha rolls, or scruff shakes. By using the methods I describe in this book, you can

train your dog to respect you by teaching him to relinquish, on your command, the resources that a leader is supposed to control. All this can be accomplished with *training*—not force, not harsh discipline.

It's true that people have dogs who refuse to obey, even after attending training classes. These out-of-control dogs more often result from a breed personality trait (discussed in Chapter 2) than from alpha dog status. Some dogs are a lot of work to train. Unlike easier-to-train dogs who have certain traits bred into them that make them want to comply to an owner's guidance, some dogs may not have a strong, inborn desire to obey their owner. With these dogs, it takes work to create a good relationship and to teach them to follow your leadership.

Many of my clients insist that they have "alpha dogs," even after I tell them that's not the problem. They say "Oh, but my dog *is* an alpha. He is pushy and insistent about getting his way. He is definitely an alpha dog." I often use the example of a working dog to try to explain how certain breed traits could be mistaken for an "alpha dog." A working Border Collie is pushy and insistent about getting his way. Let's face it: If the Border Collie politely approached a sheep and asked him to head on over to the corral, that sheep wouldn't go anywhere. Instead, the Border Collie asserts himself until he gets his way. And even if a Border Collie isn't herding sheep in his everyday life, it doesn't mean that he won't, by nature, get pushy and insistent when he wants his way. It's a trait bred into this breed, and he'll use it as a tool

Dogs will bond to a strong leader.

(sometimes on you), to get what he wants. It's up to you to teach your dog otherwise.

The truth about an alpha dog is that few problem behaviors can be attributed to this trait. People with hard-to-train dogs should not make the assumption that their dog is an "alpha" and use that as an excuse for harsh techniques. Instead, owners of hard-to-train dogs should set up good group dynamics in the household that will create great dog–human relationships.

Is There an Order to the Dog Pack?

With wolves, we see alpha, beta, omega, and other levels of hierarchy. Do dog packs work in the same way? Some controversy currently exists about how pack status affects dogs (if it does at all). Here's what I have ascertained from my experience training dogs and observing dogs in groups.

Lead or Follow?

If you were to simplify pack or group dynamics, you would find that some dogs prefer to be followers, while others will grab the opportunity to lead. The position your dog naturally assumes in a group— follower or leader—will have an effect on trainability. If your dog has an inclination to take charge, he will certainly need training and good leadership from you to learn to comply. If your dog is content to follow a leader or has no desire to lead at all, he may follow your commands—even if you show poor leadership skills.

Submissive Dogs

I've observed another level of pack order in dogs similar to that of the omega wolf—the submissive dog. These types of dogs tend to have a sneaky way of securing resources. They won't march up and try to take something they want (e.g., a bone) away from another dog. But they will wait until what they want is unattended and then take it. I think of these types of submissive dogs as being at the bottom of the pack.

Training submissive dogs can at times be problematic because they often want to offer submissive behaviors, which become counterproductive to training. For example, I've had a submissive dog roll onto his back and expose his belly when I take hold of the leash and ask for a command. To let the dog know that this isn't what I want, I turn my back, pause a moment, and then walk away. If the dog doesn't get up and follow, I will often give the leash a gentle tug to get his attention and to get him on his feet, then praise and continue on for a short walk, after which I stop and once again ask for the command.

Overly submissive dogs often benefit from confidence building to overcome training issues, which we'll discuss in detail in Chapter 9.

Troubles With Social Climbers

While most problem behaviors can't be blamed on a dog being an "alpha," problems do occur with dogs who are "social climbers" or who some people call "alpha

How Age Affects Social Climbers

With many dogs, age can influence the degree of social climbing. The problem often starts during the dog's adolescence, which can begin as early as three and a half months. Through the first three to five years of age, the urge to take over seems to be the worst. After five (sometimes six) years of age, the dog's quest to gain privileges will often taper off.

wannabes." I first heard about this concept from a seminar given by the late trainer and author Barbara Handler. Handler's theory was that some dogs get up every morning and check to see if there is a new opening at the top. In other words, some dogs have a tendency to always look for opportunities to gain more privileges. Many dogs can settle into a household once they understand the rules and who is the leader, but this is not true of the social climber. These dogs are not alpha dogs—they just want to gain control of privileges, which allows them to move up in status. From my experiences with social climbers, I know how challenging they can be.

Dealing With a Social Climber

You'll be able to deal with a social climber if you work into your routine a reminder that *you* are the one in charge. I often find feeding time a great time to do this. I'll ask for a *down*, set down a bowl of food, and have the dog wait for me to give a release word. Typically, I'll add some power to this training by having the dog look at me before I release him to go and eat. (I'll discuss power training in detail in Chapter 5.) Note that these reminders should never be harsh—they are meant to reinforce your leadership.

The bottom line is that if you have a dog who wakes up every morning looking to step into a leadership role, you may find

Training can remind a persistent social climber that you are in charge.

yourself needing to do reminders on a daily basis. The good news is that over the years, dogs tend to back off of the social climbing obsession, and reminders are needed far less often.

Group Dynamics and Leadership

Whenever you have two or more individuals interacting, you have group dynamics. To enjoy a good relationship with your dog, you need good group dynamics, which helps him know where his place is in your household.

Part of group dynamics involves individuals working out who gets what privileges and resources. Conflict arises when one or more of those individuals believe that they should have more privileges than the others. The quickest way to end this type of conflict is to have a leader who takes charge of privileges and resources. This leader must be an individual whom the other members of the group respect and are willing to follow.

For your dog to live harmoniously with you and within your group situation, you must be the leader. Part of your leadership responsibilities is to manage all the resources, such as food, toys, and where your dog sleeps. As a leader, you must teach your dog that in your group—which includes all members of the household, both human and animal—all executive decisions are yours to make. Your dog may not claim any resources without your permission. For example, if your dog is chewing a Nylabone, he must relinquish it to you when you ask for it. By making and enforcing that rule, you not only maintain your leadership position but you eliminate conflict. If you don't teach your dog to relinquish an item, he may become possessive and growl at you if you try to take it. If you fail to take away the Nylabone, he may begin to wonder what other things he doesn't have to comply with.

Let me be clear about leadership and your dog: You are not a wolf, nor is your dog, so there is no need to use the same techniques that a wolf uses to maintain order. Being a strong leader does not mean punishing your dog for anything you deem as disobedient. Instead, you must teach him the behaviors you do want. If he fails to comply, persist and insist that he do as he is told. Your dog does not need harsh punishment, but he must not be allowed to follow his behavior over yours.

There Is Harmony in Order

One of the keys to group harmony is to make sure that all the group members know their place. Animals who live in packs, such as horses, don't fight to

Like dogs, horses are pack animals with an order to their pack structure.

Many dogs won't cause you any trouble, even if you don't take charge of resources and privileges. However, a social climber or a pushier dog can become problematic if you don't bother to control the resources.

the bone or toy, who gets to eat first, and who leads whom through a doorway or on a walk. With each coveted privilege a dog manages to control, he climbs higher in pack status. Dogs of equal status may not control identical privileges but more often seem to control privileges of equivalent point values.

Problems can arise when dogs higher in pack status begin to see themselves in charge as opposed to seeing their owners in charge. Dog owners who don't establish themselves as strong leaders may find that their dogs are claiming privileges the owners have not worked to control—the kinds of privileges to which a dog awards points.

Training a dog is one way to elevate yourself into a position as your dog's leader. A leader enforces the rules, so when you require your dog to do a command—even a simple *sit*—he is learning to comply to you in a leadership role.

When your dog gets away with breaking the rules, you lose leadership points. Dogs of a lower pack status may view you as a poor leader and become sluggish or choosy about their compliance. Dogs of higher pack status and social climbers will often begin to claim more and more privileges that belong to you as a leader because you failed to enforce your authority. A dog who has gained enough points may feel bold enough to launch a coup and take over command. In extreme cases, these dogs may decide to enforce their newfound power by using aggression on other members of the household.

the death over food because the horses understand who has the higher status. While there may be some fussing around feeding time, the horses know who will end up yielding to whom in the end. Conflicts tend to arise when a new individual is introduced to the pack. Once the new member finds his place in the pecking order, the conflicts resolve. Likewise, when your dog learns his place in your household, there will be group harmony.

The Point System

Group dynamics become more difficult when two individuals want to be the leader. And just as humans have different techniques to work out this type of conflict, so do dogs. One technique is aggression. But because aggression has such dire consequences, dogs also use other methods to gain a higher status, including claiming privileges that belong to the leader. I call this the "point system."

It has been my observation that dogs seem to treat privileges as if "points" were attached. These privileges include who gets first choice of a sleeping area, who gets

Dominance, Dominating, and a Peaceful Pack

Dominance is a trait that some dogs naturally possess—it's a normal way for dogs to behave together. (This is discussed more in Chapter 2.) When a dog uses dominating tactics, he may posture over another dog, such as standing over the dog and growling, or he may use an alpha roll. Some people have tried to imitate dog techniques for dominating in an attempt to establish dominance over their dog. People who do this often feel that this is the best way to control a dog, but these techniques are often harsh and equate to bullying. I do not recommend this type of training.

Lessons From Raising Rotties

Words like "dominance" and "dominating" are often discussed in the same context with pack order and group dynamics. Following is a perspective from a woman who is raising a breed of dogs many would consider "dominant."

Dog trainer Nannette Nordenholt is the person whom Rottweiler rescue in Colorado turns to when all other options have failed. She has saved several Rottweilers whom dog professionals recommended euthanizing. According to Nannette, "dominance" is an overused word when it comes to dog behavior. Just like the "alpha" label, people are too quick to blame their dog's behavior problems on dominance, which in turn can lead to using dominating techniques on the dog. Nannette has had great success using positive training techniques on her Rottweilers, including rewarding with praise and using good dog management. Her Rottweilers taught her years ago that the old "yank-and-spank" approach to training doesn't work.

Instead of labeling her dogs "dominant," Nannette likes to see her Rottweilers as reincarnated lawyers, because "Lawyers know the rules but will often make an appeal." She compares it to a child who often checks to see if the rules have changed. Nannette doesn't feel challenged by her Rottweilers, but she knows that the breed's lawyerly side can lead to requests contrary to established rules. She will only grant appeals for privileges she feels the dog has earned. She stresses that with a Rottweiler, you need to learn to acknowledge good behaviors.

Keeping the Peace

Nannette exercises good leadership to keep the peace in her canine pack. She knows that she must sometimes give guidance to her dogs, especially if the order of the pack has been disrupted due to the introduction of a new dog, the death of an old dog, or an older dog deciding to relinquish his status to a younger member. One of the techniques Nannette uses to keep the peace is to interrupt any inappropriate eye contact, such as one dog fixating on (staring at) another dog. It's important to understand dog signals and intervene before the dog commits an unwanted action.

Another way she keeps the peace is by feeding her Rottweilers in the pack order the dogs have settled on—keeping the order of the hierarchy maintains the peace.

When it comes to pack order, Nannette allows the dogs to establish their own hierarchy—as long as the dogs do it peacefully. She follows the advice of Trish King, respected dog trainer and author of *Parenting Your Dog*, who recommends that you don't force pack order. Situations like an older dog yielding to a younger member of the pack should be allowed to happen as long as the dogs are not acting aggressively. You can't use your human perspective to decide what is "fair." "If the dogs don't have an issue with the status change," says Nannette, "then let the dogs decide, as long as this decision doesn't affect their view of you as a leader."

Be a Good Manager

Besides appreciating pack dynamics, Nannette's Rotties have taught her to be a good dog manager. Training is always the foundation when starting a relationship with a new pack member. She uses "active supervision" when introducing a new dog to her pack—which is not the same as just being in the household with a dog. It requires keeping an active watch for unwanted activities. "You can't let some of the dogs play excessively if that play is irritating more established members of the

Rottweilers, who often get labeled as dominant, respond to good leadership and consistent training.

pack," she says. "Some dogs become cranky when young ones get too rambunctious, and that can turn into a fight."

Establishing boundaries and not allowing the new dog to ignore you are all part of her management program. Nanette teaches her Rottweilers that engaging in good behaviors earns them privileges, like getting to sleep in her bedroom. Implementing good pack management, training, positive reinforcement, and structure helped establish her as a leader—not dominating techniques or harsh discipline.

Chapter Two

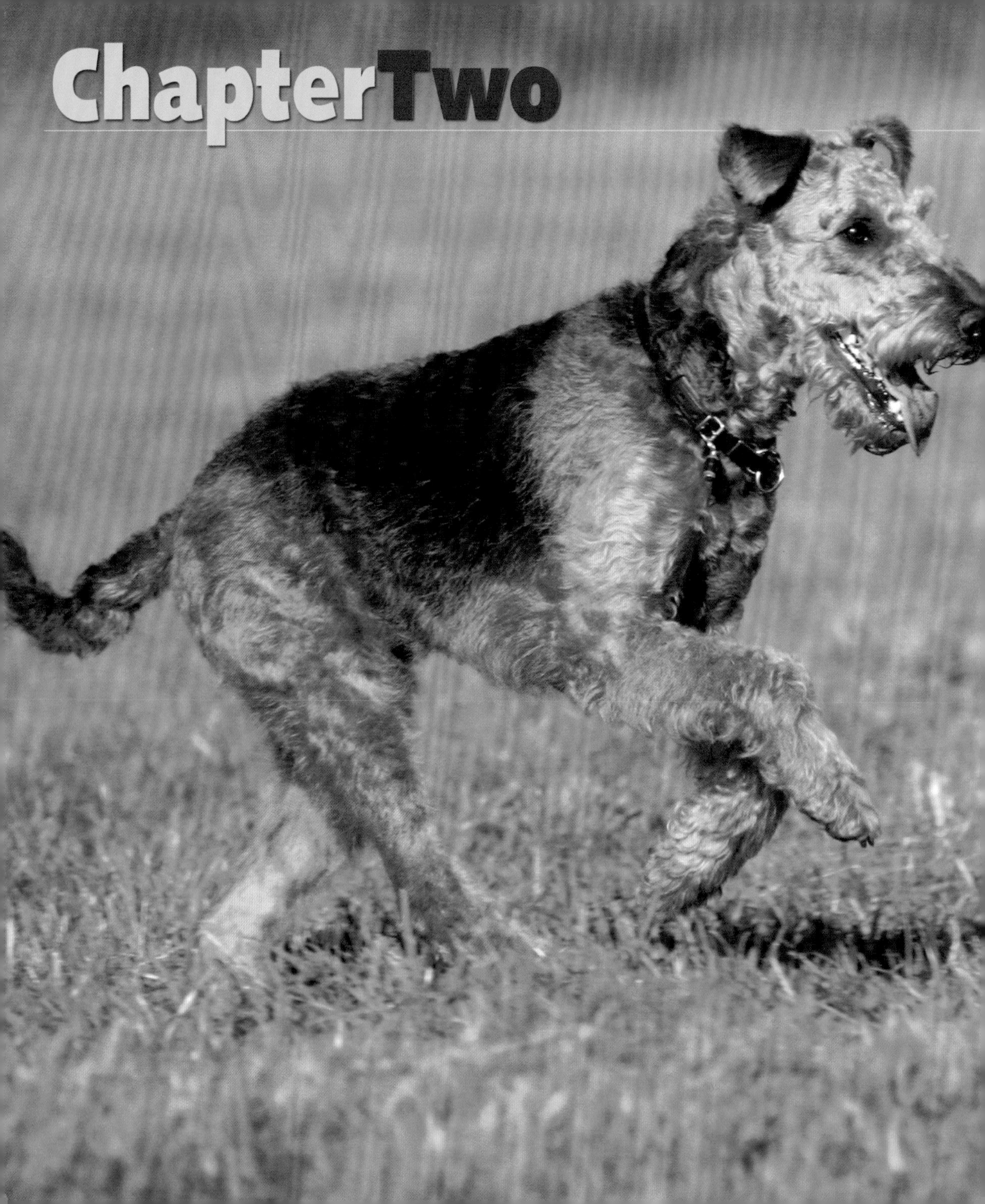

Traits That Make a Dog More Difficult to Train

In general, I find that there are two main factors that go into making a dog harder to train. The first is certain breed characteristics that are incompatible with following your commands. The second is pack status and how a dog relates to the group dynamics in your home. Sometimes difficulties arise from just one of these issues, while sometimes it's a combination of both.

After a discussion of breed characteristics and pack status, I take a look at some of the breed characteristics that can make training more difficult. To make the concepts more manageable, they've been broken down into three general groups. However, this does not mean that certain traits can't fall into other groups or that one dog can't have several traits across different groups.

Breed Characteristics and Trainability

We live in a world with a great diversity of dog breeds. Dogs have been selectively bred with certain characteristics to meet specific needs. Some traits are chosen for doing a certain type of work, like working Border Collies who are bred with attention to natural instinct, physical talent, and mental acuity to herd sheep. Some traits are chosen for protection, like certain lines of German Shepherds who are selectively bred for their guard-dog abilities. And other breeds, like the Maltese, are bred for traits that make them excellent companion dogs.

Some of these traits, which often define the breed, will affect the amount of exercise a dog requires or what kind of pet a dog will make. They can also make a difference in the trainability of a dog. Certain traits will make a dog easy to train, while other traits do not accommodate training, which creates the need for extra work to make the dog more manageable. Keep in mind that because of the great diversity in dog breeds, no one technique exists that will effectively train all dogs. Understanding

your dog's traits and adjusting your training and management techniques to his specific needs will go a long way toward helping to solve problems.

Pack Politics and Trainability

"Pack status" is the term we give the hierarchy of a group of dogs. Although wolves have a very structured pack order, the effects of pack hierarchy are more diluted in dogs. How diluted that effect is often varies with different breeds. Although I believe that pack status does affect a dog's trainability and behaviors, it is only one of several influencing factors.

As a part of a human household, a dog wants to find his place with regard to hierarchy. The goal of a hierarchy in any group is to maintain peace and productivity. In a household that has one or more dogs, the ideal hierarchy is the human taking on the leadership position. People who let dogs take on leadership responsibilities in a household typically end up with dogs who have problem behaviors.

As far as pack hierarchy goes, often the most problematic dog is the social climber. (See Chapter 1.) The social climber is always looking for ways to move up in status and is likely to test an owner's leadership.

Another situation that can create a disruption in a household is when two dogs are near the top of the pack hierarchy and fairly equal in pack status. When two dogs feel competitive about their place in the pack, fights can break out over resources. This is why it's essential for you, as the

Working Breeds

A Jack Russell Terrier was bred to go into a fox den, and without any help or guidance from his owner, he will work independently until he accomplishes his mission. This dog must be willing to keep on task, even if the fox hurts him, until the task is accomplished. Sighthounds, such as a Greyhound and Afghan Hound, have been bred with the ability to spot a deer or other animal and react in a split second, sending them from an at-ease state to an all-out run in the blink of an eye. German Shepherds are bred with a drive to instinctively want to bark and bite people whom they deem threatening. This allows them to be taught to help bring down the bad guy when doing police work. They are also bred to quit an attack and calm down with a single command from their handler.

Dogs bred for different kinds of work have had certain traits so strongly bred into them that pack hierarchy takes a backseat to their predominant drive. What this means to dog owners working to train their dogs is that the techniques they use must go beyond the "alpha of the pack" concept to achieve success.

leader, to control all the resources. Dogs at the lower end of the hierarchy are typically not as problematic—at least not about fighting over resources and working to gain control—because they often want to shrink away from taking charge.

To keep peace and harmony in your household, you must understand how pack politics affect your dog's behavior and ensure that you are a good leader. Unfortunately, some breed traits work against their owners taking charge and can make training very difficult.

Group One: "Control Freaks"

The traits in this section all tend to lead to one outcome—your dog trying to

control you. Chapter 7 has more detailed information on managing and training these types of dogs.

Arrogance/High Degree of Self-Importance

While arrogance and self-importance are perhaps more about human perception, I use these terms as a way to describe a certain attitude some dogs take on. Dogs with a high degree of self-importance can become brazen about ignoring their owner's commands because it can be difficult to convince them of who's in charge. An arrogant dog has the attitude that his decisions, thoughts, and actions should take precedence over any other, which means that he's more likely to want to do things his way. The more he is allowed to ignore your commands, the less like a leader you appear in his eyes.

Effects of Pack Status

Often, dogs of higher pack status have a sense of arrogance or self-importance. This kind of attitude is often developed by dogs who feel quite at home with deciding what to do and what not to do, without any input from their owner.

Breed Characteristics

In general, this trait seems to be more prevalent in working breeds whose activities help build a sense of self-importance through independent decision making. Dogs who are allowed more take-charge opportunities by the nature of what they

Herding dogs such as the Australian Shepherd (left), guard dogs such as the Great Pyrenees (center), and terriers such as the West Highland White Terrier (bottom right) may all have a high degree of self-importance.

were bred to do are more prone to having a high degree of self-importance. Sometimes this happens with herding dogs, like Border Collies and Australian Shepherds, who make their own decisions when working. Dogs who are bred to work quarry, like many terriers, can have this trait because they often must make decisions without any guidance from their owners. It's also natural for some guard dogs, like the Great Pyrenees, to work without guidance. For a dog to do these kinds of jobs, he must possess a sense of self-importance, which allows him to make take-charge decisions.

Training Issues

An owner of a dog with a bit too much self-importance may need to do some extra rehearsals on the dog's obedience training. The dog needs to be taught to focus in on his owner's commands instead of his own wishes. Good leadership is essential, because self-importance can become a vicious cycle—the more a self-important dog blows off commands, the more self-important he'll become, which leads to an even greater lack of compliance.

Another good way to counter this problem is to form a strong bond with the dog, which can help convince him to do his owner's bidding over his own desires. Positive, reward-based training will help form a close relationship and help the dog choose his owner's way over his way. Punishment for noncompliance will only distance the dog from his owner.

Leadership

Unlike wolves, not all dogs will concern themselves with having to have a strong leader. This is not to say that being a good leader for your dog isn't what you should strive for, but some dogs can exist amiably with owners who are poor leaders.

Assertive/Demanding

An assertive nature is the tendency to want to take action on something the dog feels good about. For example, some dogs take up chasing animals, bicycles, or cars and won't listen when their owners try to get them to stop. If you find your dog constantly engaging in behaviors that you have already trained him not to do, you probably have a more assertive dog.

Assertive dogs can become very demanding. They will use pawing, barking, repetitive jumping, and sometimes nipping to get their way. Because these dogs are often highly creative, unwanted behaviors are usually a result, especially when they are bored.

Effects of Pack Status

Alpha dogs are naturally assertive, although some are more assertive than others. Dogs who are high in pack status can also become very assertive about getting their way. However, dogs of high pack status will not always be the most assertive dogs—this trait can appear in any dog of any pack level, especially if it's a breed trait.

Assertive or Dominant?

Some people confuse an assertive nature (the tendency to want to take action on something the dog feels good about) with a dominant nature (the tendency to want to be in charge and make decisions) because both dominant and assertive dogs can use a lot of effort when working to get their way. Both dominant and highly assertive dogs can come across as very pushy.

Breed Characteristics

Assertiveness is a strong trait in many working breeds, no matter what their pack status may be. Herding breeds, such as the Border Collies and Australian Shepherds, and hunting breeds that directly encounter quarry, such as Jack Russell Terriers and Dachshunds, are typically more assertive. But an assertive nature can still vary from mild to very strong within any breed.

Training Issues

An assertive dog is a true training challenge, even more so than a dominant dog. You can train the assertive dog endlessly and have him respect you as a leader, but you can't train him to stop continually trying to assert his will or creatively trying to get his way. An assertive dog is even more of a challenge when he has a high sense of self-importance. When a difference of opinion arises between dog and owner, the dog with high self-importance will want to do things his way, even though he acknowledges his owner as the leader.

Dominant

Dominance may perhaps be one of the most overused labels on which dog behaviors are blamed. This catch-all term sends people looking for the wrong solution to their dog's behavior issues. Although dominance is a trait that occurs in some dogs, it's too quickly applied to any dog who misbehaves. This often leads to the excuse of using unnecessary "dominating" techniques on these dogs.

A truly dominant nature is a nature that empowers an individual to feel quite comfortable with making decisions. This results in a dog with an attitude of authority who is at home making leadership decisions. Depending on what

Jack and Parson Russell Terriers tend to be assertive breeds.

other strong traits a dominant dog has, he may be somewhat forceful when seeing through these decisions. For example, a dominant dog who is highly assertive will work a little harder than a less assertive dog to make sure that his subordinates do what he decides. Not all dominant dogs are forceful about making leadership choices. In fact, many dominant dogs would be quite content if their owners took charge. However, if the owner doesn't take command, the dog will.

Many people think that dominance is synonymous with aggression. However, aggression is merely a tool some dogs employ to assert their dominance. Aggression is used for many other reasons, including fear, protection, and predatory drives.

Effects of Pack Status

Dominance is a characteristic that belongs to the alpha dog of any breed and can also be seen in dogs of higher pack status. However, some dog breeds have dominance as a breed trait, which means that dogs of any level of pack status may show some degree of it.

Breed Characteristics

Some breeds that have dominance as a breed trait include "bully" breeds such as Bulldogs and Rottweilers. There is a greater tendency for guard dog breeds, like the Great Pyrenees and Bullmastiff, to have dominant individuals.

Training Issues

Strong leadership skills are the best way to manage a more dominant dog, and training is the best way to get a dominant dog to see his owner as the leader. An owner will also

Bulldogs (right) and Bullmastiffs (below) may tend toward dominating behaviors.

have to take control of the resources, such as the sleeping areas, food, attention, and play.

Without training, a more dominant dog may take charge and decide which people are allowed in the house (which the dog sees as his den), attack other dogs in the household, or bite when the owner tries to touch his food or discipline him. Dominant dogs who are allowed to take charge of these and other issues can become dangerous because their nature makes them want to enforce their authority.

High Drive

By definition, drive is a strong urge and desire to *do*, to press onward forcibly, usually excessively. A dog with a high drive will overcome any opposition to accomplish what he is driven to do. Some dogs have a high drive to comply to training. (These dogs are often selected for service work.) However, if the dog's high drive is not directed to training, difficulty can ensue. A Beagle with a high drive to hunt will abandon an agility run if he catches the scent of something he feels he must pursue. A sighthound will take off full speed in pursuit of a rabbit he sees in a field. A Jack Russell will endlessly jump at a window if he sees a fox cross the road. High drive puts a dog into action but not always the action the owner wants.

Breed Characteristics

High drive can be present in many breeds, but terriers and herding dogs are the prime examples of this trait.

Persistent Terriers

The higher the dog's drive, the more likely he is to pursue that drive, even at a high personal cost. Take for instance Tuffy, a Jack Russell Terrier. He was inside a den working to draw out a raccoon. When he finally flushed out the raccoon, he emerged with two gashes on his head that required stitches. Tuffy's drive to accomplish his task kept him from retreating—even when painfully injured. Although Tuffy sustained pain while performing the task, his high drive to achieve caused him to persist.

Tuffy will, however, try to find a way to keep from getting hurt the next time. A dog who takes action to prevent unwanted consequences is using avoidance behavior. Although all dogs use avoidance behavior to some extent, some do so with greater expertise. Many high-drive dogs who will persist in a task regardless of pain or other discouragement excel at using avoidance behavior. This is why punishment is not the best way to train these dogs. Instead of changing his behavior to avoid getting punished, the dog is more likely to decide that if he avoids getting caught, then he can avoid the punishment—and continue doing what he wants.

Herding Dogs

I once heard an owner who'd just paid a large vet bill say "You'd think the dog would learn after the horse kicked him in the head. But no, as soon as the vet removed the stitches, the dog went right back to chasing."

Chasing is a common problem with some dogs, especially herding breeds like Border Collies and Australian Cattle Dogs. They naturally want to run after and nip livestock. Some also see cars, bicycles, running children, and even running adults as enticement. However, even when the dog sustains an injury from being kicked by the livestock or by chasing, it isn't unusual for him to continue engaging in the exact same behavior. Dogs with a high drive often stay committed to their task. When that task is to please their owner, the owner is happy; when that task is to chase, the owner may not be so pleased. Problems occur when the dog's drive goes beyond a natural sense of self-survival and he persists, ignoring pain to accomplish the task.

While high drive can be present in many breeds, terriers (like this Fox Terrier, right) and herding dogs (like this Border Collie, center) are prime examples.

Dogs in High-Drive Mode

Dogs in high drive can have a very intense focus as they become completely absorbed with the task at hand. A dog who is in high drive can block out other stimuli. He will not react to pain until later and will often not hear calls from his owner because he is so focused on the task at hand.

Herding dogs are selectively bred to not quit a job, even if injured. If a good herding dog gave up when he was hurt, years of training would be lost. The dogs who were willing to overcome fear, pain, and other adversities to accomplish the task were selected because they were more likely to succeed at their job. And while these traits make a great working dog, some of them cause pet owners grief.

Training Issues

Because these dogs will persist in doing a task even when hurt, inflicting punishment to stop unwanted behaviors doesn't work. High-drive dogs can also be highly sensitive (see page 34), and using harsh methods will affect bonding. You'll end up with a dog who cowers but still misbehaves.

Independent

Independent dogs are comfortable "doing their own thing" without any guidance from their owners. While an independent dog can love his owner, there's a lack of a drive to please anyone. When something arises that interests the dog, he'll pursue that interest with little or no regard to his owner.

I've placed independent dogs in this group because their nature makes them want to be in charge of themselves. This creates the same kinds of problems—and resolutions— as with dominant and assertive dogs.

Breed Characteristics

Independent traits are often found in terriers, certain hunting breeds such as the Saluki, and some of the northern breeds such as Huskies and Malamutes. Basenjis can also be independent.

Training Issues

Independent dogs need a lot of training to focus in on their owners. Basic training and power training (see Chapters 4 and 5) will help the independent dog look to his owner for guidance as he learns to follow his owner's commands over his own will.

Group Two: "Stubborn as a Mule"

These traits tend to lead to a stubborn dog who refuses to comply or who has intermittent compliance. Chapter 8 has more detailed information about reforming stubborn dogs.

Independent

The independent trait also belongs in this group because with independent dogs, a strong will can often lead to stubbornness. These dogs can also have a strong sense of self-importance, making them even more likely to pursue their goals over those of their owners.

Breed Characteristics

As noted earlier, terriers, certain hunting breeds, and northern breeds tend to be independent, which leads to stuborness.

Training

Because independent dogs are so comfortable working without any guidance from their owners, disharmony can result in a human household. To counter the independent dog's tendency not to naturally look to his owner for guidance, he needs training, which can teach him compliance.

Because independent dogs often have less interest in doing their owner's bidding, the owner will find that her dog becomes quickly distracted during training sessions. Although shorter training sessions can help, these dogs need training to extend their attention span for tasks they would normally deem uninteresting.

Strong Willed/Stubborn

There is a subtle difference between strong willed and stubborn, and both can be very problematic. "Strong willed" is often associated with a dog who isn't easily deterred from the task at hand. Sometimes a strong-willed dog is driven by urges

that are bred into him, such as the urge to pursue a running animal or to kill a rodent. "Stubborn" is often associated with a dog who only chooses to comply to certain tasks, mostly those that are self-fulfilling.

Huskies (below) and Salukis (right) can have independent traits.

Breed Characteristics

Stubbornness and a strong will are often found in the more independent breeds. Some of the northern breeds, such as the Shiba Inu, can have these traits. Italian Greyhounds might be considered submissive but will show a stubborn streak at times. A lot of the more assertive dogs, such as Australian Shepherds, can be strong willed about getting their way, and some will be downright stubborn. Terriers are the poster children for stubbornness.

Training Issues

Stubbornness and a strong will can seem to replace a drive for compliance. Although some dogs will comply with their owners with little or no question as to why they should, a stubborn dog must first understand what benefits compliance brings.

Using the wrong technique on these dogs can be disastrous because harsh methods can actually increase stubbornness. The secret to successfully training a more stubborn dog is to realize that you can't force compliance—instead, you must find a

Shiba Inu (left) and Italian Greyhounds (below) can have stubborn streaks.

way to teach the dog that compliance is in his best interest. Although this isn't an easy task, the best way to gain compliance is to start with the simple things first, like your basic commands, using rewards to keep the dog more motivated. Then, work up to issues where the dog is going to be more resistant. You may find that you need to do your training in an undistracted area and eventually work up to a more distracting environment until compliance becomes a habit. With a stubborn or strong-willed dog, you need to keep lessons short. Reward frequently and immediately, choosing something the dog is strongly invested in as a reward.

Group Three: "Nervous Nellies"

The traits in this section tend to lead to a more nervous dog. Dogs with extra sensitivity require special handling when training, which is discussed in detail in Chapter 9.

Bullying

Bullying and punishment have more drawbacks than benefits when used on any kind of dog. Although some dogs may learn to comply with that kind of training, punishment and bullying destroy an owner's bond with her dog. Bonding can be a key factor in driving compliance when that desire isn't naturally bred into the dog.

High Distractibility

High distractibility is the tendency for a dog to divert his attention from his owner or his owner's command and take up another mission.

Breed Characteristics

Sighthounds, like Greyhounds and Salukis, by nature want to run after moving prey and often find looking off in the distance more appealing than keeping an eye on their owners. Scenthounds, such as Beagles, can become highly distracted by scents. It doesn't take long for these dogs' noses to lower to the ground. When scents distract them, they lose focus. Even Golden Retrievers, at times, can be easily distracted. It may be because Goldens were originally bred to work fowl, and catching slight movements in the brush can be an advantage for a hunting dog. Goldens who are far removed from their hunting roots may not retain this trait, while others may display it more strongly.

Training Issues

Highly distractible breeds can be quite challenging to train. Their attention is often diverted from their owner, causing them to miss a command. Control of these dogs can be easily lost when the focus is not on the owner. Start as young as you can with positive training if you have a highly distractible dog. You will need to use exercises designed to focus his attention, like *watch me*, found in Chapter 4.

Greyhounds, who by nature want to run after moving prey, can be highly distractible.

Highly Reactive/Sensitive

A highly reactive dog will react to stimuli in his environment that other dogs see as benign. Just raise your hand and a highly reactive dog may crouch or jump away. People who own highly reactive dogs will find that they overreact to common noises and events that other dogs seem to ignore. For example, a highly reactive dog may become shaken by the noise of a soda can rattling out of a vending machine. Once the dog overreacts, he may continue to become more and more unnerved.

A sensitive nature creates a higher degree of reactivity in a dog. While sensitivity in dogs can be positive, such as dogs who can sense oncoming seizures in people, high sensitivity can have drawbacks, such as reacting negatively to an owner's stress level or nerves.

Breed Characteristics

When it comes to high reactivity, some herding dogs react to the slightest movement, which comes in handy when an animal makes an unexpected move that could endanger the dog. These dogs seem to react instantaneously and without thought—which is a great trait to have if a horse happens to jump unexpectedly when the dog is working but a problem if he's constantly overreacting at home or when training.

When it comes to highly sensitive breeds, many people are surprised that some of the more dominant breeds fall into this category. Bulldogs, French Bulldogs, and Rottweilers are all quite sensitive. Jack Russell Terriers, Italian Greyhounds, and Border Collies can also be on the sensitive side.

Training Issues

Sensitive dogs tend to react strongly to harsh treatment. A highly sensitive dog may react poorly to reprimands given by an owner, even if the reprimand is only a harsher tone of voice. Positive training techniques are especially important when dealing with a more sensitive dog, and any reprimands must be kept low key and to a minimum.

Dogs who are highly sensitive will often shut down from harsh treatment. For example, a sensitive dog who's reluctant to heel will not learn to comply if his owner jerks the lead harshly to correct him. Instead, this treatment will cause him to crouch and drag from a harsh jerk (shut down). Using a treat to lure the dog to keep up and then rewarding him for the correct behavior is a much more positive method.

Dog owners must work to desensitize and build confidence in dogs who overreact to benign events. When handled correctly and positively, highly reactive dogs tend to desensitize to their owners and cultivate a working

You may be surprised that French Bulldogs (right) and Rottweilers (below) are both sensitive breeds.

Dominant and Sensitive

Many people experience training issues when a dog has an overly sensitive personality paired with a dominant nature. (See page 26.) It may be hard to picture a dominant dog as sensitive. After all, these dogs are often bold and persistent about getting their way. However, dominant dogs can be highly sensitive, adding to the difficulty in training them.

Although a dominant dog needs training by his owner to maintain control, using harsh techniques can be disastrous. Physically correcting a dominant but highly sensitive dog can cause him to react aggressively, and he may not hesitate in defending himself against the punishment by biting. Plus, harsher training techniques will damage the valuable human–dog bond.

relationship with them. Practicing basic obedience helps create a less reactive dog because he learns to better read his owner's actions and cues.

Low Impulse Control

Impulse control deals with a dog's thought processes. A dog who has low impulse control will do very little thinking before taking action. Dogs with more impulse control will think about the stimuli, then make a decision, and finally take action. These dogs give off subtle cues before they act that allows their owners time to redirect their attention. Dogs with low impulse control tend to act more immediately. One minute an Italian Greyhound may be prancing alongside his owner, then in an instant he may be racing off across a field because a rabbit caught his attention. The action had almost no warning, leaving his owner no time to stop it.

Breed Characteristics

Sighthounds, such as the Greyhound, Afghan Hound, and Whippet, are often characterized by low impulse control. Sighthounds are renowned for going from a peaceful, inattentive state of mind to a full-out run toward game—all in the blink of an eye.

Training Issues

Typically, intercepting an action before the dog commits it is the best way to successfully change unwanted behavior. Low impulse control doesn't allow the luxury of an owner being able to "read the dog." Making this issue all the more of a challenge is that dogs in impulse mode tend to shut out all other stimuli and focus on the task at hand. This can block out any commands given by an owner when the dog is engaged in an unwanted behavior.

Training dogs who have low impulse control can take a lot of creativity. Good management, including keeping the dog on leash, can help prevent issues. Training the dog to focus on the owner by using the *watch me* command (see Chapter 4) and by building a strong bond will help build canine confidence and instill more impulse control.

Shy

Some dogs are shy by nature, and the degree of shyness can range from reserved to very shy. A reserved dog doesn't run up to greet strange people or strange dogs; he prefers to take things slowly. Reserved dogs will want to approach a stranger rather than be approached. A very shy dog will try to withdraw from people or dogs they don't

Good Temperament

An even temperament makes a dog easier to train and more stable. A good temperament means that the dog isn't shy, skittish, overreactive, or overly sensitive. Typically, an even-tempered dog is confident around strange people and strange dogs. Most even-tempered dogs do not react aggressively when dealing with adversity.

know. These dogs will not want to approach others at all.

Sighthounds, such as the Afghan Hound, are often trademarked by low impulse control.

Border Collies have a tendency toward shyness.

Socializing a shyer dog can take a lot of work. Progress can be slow, and the dog may never feel completely comfortable around unknown people or dogs. Some dogs may be selectively shy, reacting to certain kinds of dogs, small children, or certain men or women.

Effects of Pack Status

Shyness is often associated with dogs who are lower in pack status but is not limited to those dogs.

Breed Characteristics

Border Collies have a tendency toward shyness, which may be due to the fact that they were bred and kept on farms with little interaction with people outside their family. Some Jack Russell Terriers can be shy, even when socialized. With some shyer breeds, like Dalmatians and Pharaoh Hounds, early socialization can make a great difference. Other more reserved breeds include Shelties, Greyhounds, and Bouviers des Flandres.

Training Issues

When shown good leadership, some shy dogs can be easy to train in basic obedience because they tend to depend more on their owners. However, working to socialize a shyer dog can become a task unto itself, which can take away from other training time.

Three Universal Training Tips

In this chapter, we discuss several traits that can make a dog more difficult to train. As different as some of those traits are, there are several general training suggestions that I've found can work for almost any dog:

1. Control the resources. For example, incorporate training into your dog's feeding routine. Ask for a sit-stay before you put down the food bowl, and don't let your dog go to it until you give the release word. This helps you establish yourself as a leader because you are controlling an important resource—food.

2. Avoid punishment. Harsh techniques are not useful—even for a dog considered dominant or stubborn. They will inevitably cause more problem behaviors than they solve.

3. Develop a strong bond. Developing a strong bond with your dog will encourage him to look to you for guidance and establish yourself as a leader. This is another reason not to use punishment, which destroys that valuable bond between you and your dog.

We'll delve further into these concepts in the training sections of this book.

Chapter Three

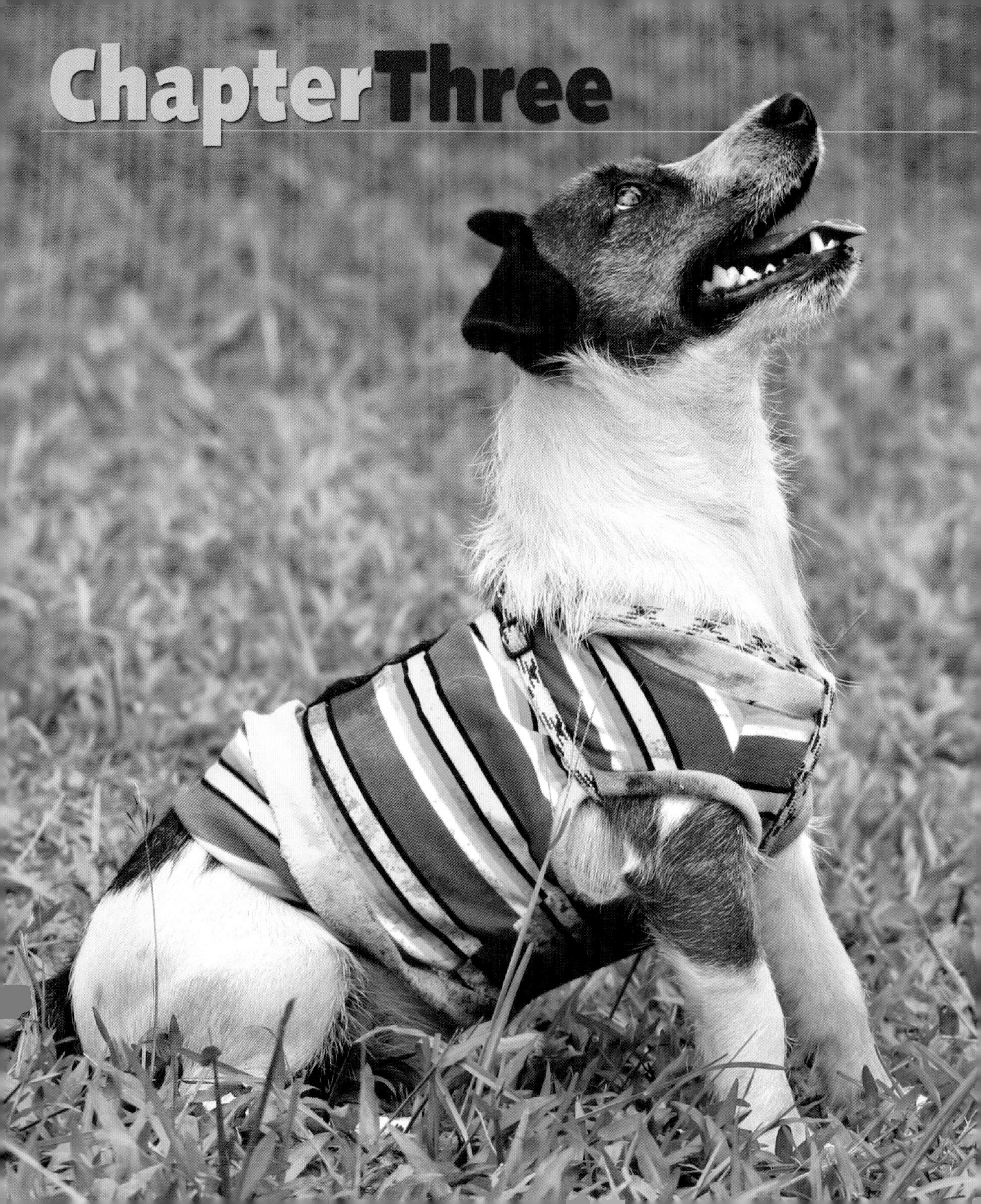

Principles of Learning, General Training Rules, and Training Precautions

Training can help with the cultural differences between people and dogs. Training teaches dogs boundaries, like don't eliminate in the house and stay away from that food on the table. Good training not only teaches your dog what you want him to do, but it puts you in a leadership role because your dog learns to look to you for guidance.

Over the years, dog trainers have learned that there are ways to make training a dog easier. Understanding how a dog learns will benefit you greatly, as will following some general training guidelines that explain the subtle techniques that more experienced dog trainers use. You'll also learn to avoid certain techniques that will inhibit or destroy training efforts.

How Dogs Learn

From the moment a dog is born, he must learn in order to survive. A young puppy is dependent on his mother to survive and is also in a stage where he will learn in a dependent mode, a mode in which he will accept direction without question. As the dog grows, much like with people, his brain will rewire itself as he transitions into an adult—some people refer to this time as canine adolescence. Here, the dog goes from a dependent learner to an independent learner. Although some dog breeds learn with the willingness of a puppy throughout their lives, others have more of a tendency to not automatically accept what they are taught once they mature.

Puppies Are Dependent Learners

Puppies are at a great age to begin training. Good dog breeders will actually begin to train a pup before you take him home by handling him, working with his mouth, and manipulating his paws. When handled correctly, puppies will build trust and bond to people. For the first three to four months of life, a dog will naturally follow a leader.

Puppies are dependent learners.

Adolescents and Adults Are Independent Learners

Sometime around the age of three and a half months and onward, a dog's mind begins to change. When that change is complete, he will no longer follow without thinking—his mind has rewired from the dependent puppy to the independent adult.

During adolescence, a dog makes the transition from dependent learner, or one who complies without question, to an individual who thinks before he complies. Some of the more independent breeds question commands at a much earlier age and may not seem to have much of a dependent stage at all.

For some dogs, adolescence can be filled with turmoil, while others have a smooth transition. With most, the worst behavior is seen between about four months of age through the first year. During this time, a dog begins to spar for position in the pack. To find his place, he will test his limits. A dog who has no leadership from his owner may decide to take charge of the household. Even a dog who has some training may begin to try to claim different privileges. He may decide to growl if someone tries to get him to move, or he will protect his food. The dog that once happily came when called will now look at his owner as if to say "Who said you were the boss?" Complicating the matter is that not all dogs go through the brain-rewiring process smoothly. Some dogs will be aggressive one moment and show submission the next—they'll snap at you to assert themselves, then submissively urinate after a reprimand. Between five and eight months of age, dogs can become fearful of strangers, especially men and children, creating a need for continued socialization.

Behavioral Changes After the First Year

With good training, a lot of dogs will settle down after their first year. Although the

Take a Class

If you own a puppy, go to a puppy class. This not only helps get your dog trained but also socializes him and offers an opportunity to train him in a distracting area. But don't stop at a puppy class—dogs greatly benefit by attending a second class right after puppy class. While your dog is in early adolescence, he needs this kind of structured training and interaction with other dogs.

rewiring of the brain no longer creates the erratic behaviors seen in some dogs under a year of age, the dog is still changing his behaviors with regard to pack status and privileges. People with dominant dogs will notice that they will take major steps to gain control for a few more years. Canine dominance aggression typically develops at social maturity, which usually occurs between 18 and 36 months of age.

Training Versus Habit Formation

Habit is the process of doing something without the conscious thought of what is being done. A dog who is in the habit of coming when called will stop what he is doing and head toward the person giving the command. A dog who isn't in the habit of coming on command will think about coming and may decide that there is really nothing to gain by complying.

You can teach your dog to sit quickly, but it takes practice to get him to do a *sit* promptly and every time you give the

For some dogs, adolescence can be a time filled with erratic behaviors.

command. Training typically doesn't take a lot of time, but habit formation does. How long each dog takes to create a habit will vary with his personality and age. Compliance issues can act as a roadblock to learning and habit formation.

A dog who has a high drive for compliance (also referred to as hardwired to please) typically complies because he feels that this is the right thing to do. That trait is bred into the dog, and these kinds of dogs see compliance as self-rewarding. A more independent dog will not have this same drive, although he can learn how to comply though training. Once he learns to comply,

he will get into the habit of complying rather than the habit of following his own will.

Training Methods

Over the years, my training philosophy has grown and changed. I feel that the best way to train a dog is to work as positively as possible. I do this by finding ways to train the dog to do what I want instead of punishing behaviors I don't want. Even when it is necessary to correct misbehaviors, it's important to keep the reform effort as positive as possible, simply because punishment can be destructive to the dog–human bond. With hard-to-train dogs who don't have a natural drive to comply, the human–dog relationship and bonding are what substitute for that natural compliance drive. The more positive you keep your training, the better your relationship with your dog.

At times, dogs will take up behaviors we don't want. The sooner those behaviors are addressed, the more easily the dog can be redirected to an appropriate behavior. For example, I make sure that I begin training my dogs not to chase horses before I even bring them on my property. I have someone run a horse in front of the dog, and if he tries to give chase, I use the leash to prevent the behavior and then to redirect him into a behavior I can reward, such as a *sit*. If I allowed the dog to chase the horse, tried to call him back with the *come* command, and failed, he would discover just how fun it could be to refuse to follow the command.

A good way to train most dogs is with treats.

If I swatted my dog for chasing the horse, he would then have to decide if the fun was worth the punishment, and many herding and high-drive dogs will chase even when they know that they will be punished. It's much better to find ways to train a dog and reform unwanted behaviors without getting into the punishment cycle—which may not even be effective.

Terms

There are many technical terms when it comes to training. While this book is not meant to be a scientific treatise on behavior or training, there are some terms that can be useful when discussing how best to train a hard-to-train dog.

- **Command:** A verbal cue given to a dog to elicit a specific response.
- **Correction:** An action taken to stop, discourage, or intercept an unwanted behavior.
- **Cue:** A signal given to your dog to elicit a specific behavior or response. The reaction to a cue is the result of you teaching your dog to associate that cue with a trained response.
- **Extinction:** This is when a behavior occurs with less and less frequency until the behavior ceases. Although some people think of bad behavior as finally stopping, good behaviors can also cease when not reinforced.
- **Marking a behavior:** Giving a signal to acknowledge a desired behavior the instant it happens. To mark a behavior, you can use a specific word such as "good" or "okay." Some people use a device called a clicker.
- **Negative reinforcement:** This is an action that results in taking away something the dog wants or awarding something undesirable. The undesirable award doesn't necessarily need to be harsh or equate to punishment to be effective. The goal is to extinguish an unwanted behavior.
- **Positive reinforcement:** This is the action of rewarding a desired behavior. Some possible rewards include

praise, food, play, or letting the dog do something he wants to do. The best reward is one that the dog deems worthy, not one that the owner feels is the most valuable. The goal is to encourage a wanted behavior.

- **Punishment:** A consequence that causes a behavior to occur with less frequency. Many people equate punishment with a physically harsh consequence. Some people consider punishment to mean any negative action. The goal is to stop unwanted behavior.
- **Reinforcement:** A consequence that causes a behavior to occur with more frequency.
- **Reward:** Something you do or give that the dog feels positive about, as a result of a behavior you want to reinforce. A treat can be a reward, as can petting or playing with the dog.
- **Shaping:** Shaping is a process in which you break down a desired behavior into tiny increments. Each increment is rewarded, using treats or some kind of encouragement, in order to work toward that final behavior. The example on page 77-79 uses a shaping technique to teach a dog to go from looking away from food in your hand to finally making sustained eye contact.
- **Treat training:** Using food treats as a reward when working to train a response to commands or to train a new behavior.

Play can be used to reward your dog.

Rewards Versus Negative Reinforcement

You can use many tools to train a dog, each with pitfalls and strengths. Punishment is a tool that requires a lot of training to use correctly, and when used incorrectly, can have terrible consequences. Harsh punishment can also harm the dog–human bond, which is why this book doesn't promote that kind of punishment for training a dog.

Controversy surrounds treat training, which is often employed by people looking for positive reinforcement of dog behaviors. Some people worry that training with treats can equate to bribing a dog, and sometimes it can. Correcting a dog also brings controversy. Some people argue that you must never correct a dog, and you should only use positive reinforcement and never anything else. In my experience, I have occasionally found that a correction or some kind of negative consequence is necessary or can help speed up change. However, especially with an overly sensitive dog, you should strive to do most of your training through positive reinforcement. Although you can use negative reinforcement to train a lot of different dogs, these methods are best left to discourage misbehavior rather than to shape wanted behavior.

The History of Punishment and Negative Reinforcement in Training

Punishment and negative reinforcement-based training became popular after World War II. The poster child for this type of training was the German Shepherd Dog fitted with a choke collar. Choke collars were (and still are) chain collars designed to tighten when pulled. When the chain tightened, the collar closed down on the dog's neck in a choking fashion. The belief was that this would stop or discourage unwanted behaviors or teach the dog how to comply to a command. For example, a dog would be

The Reform of Punishment and Negative Reinforcement-Based Training

Dr. Ian Dunbar is credited with beginning the turnaround from punishment and negative reinforcement training to reward-based training. Dunbar sought compliance from dogs through positive training methods. Another training pioneer, Karen Prior, introduced pet owners to the benefits of clicker training, a technique that uses a reward-based system.

told to sit. The choke collar would then be tightened with an upward pull. When the dog finally figured out that he needed to plant his back end, the choking would stop.

Likewise, when unwanted behaviors occurred, the dog owner would jerk on the choke collar. If the dog didn't comply from the jerking, the chain was sometimes pulled into a choke until the dog's breathing was compromised. The hope was that the consequences of disobeying would be uncomfortable or painful. Unfortunately, these punishment-based training techniques still persist today.

This "do as you are told or face the consequences" idea worked to train some dogs—especially the more compliant ones—but at a price. Whenever you use unnecessary force with a dog, you damage

Punishment Just Doesn't Work

There are many reasons not to use punishment, but the fact that it just doesn't work with certain types of dogs is a good reason not to use it. Take for example an assertive dog who is misbehaving or acting on impulse. This type of dog can be very sensitive and will become too rattled or stressed out by the punishment, destroying precious bonding with his owner. And because this dog by nature is bred to continue with his mission regardless of physical punishment, it's unlikely to discourage unwanted behaviors.

the human–dog bond. When you seek to train a dog to do something you want, punishment is not the right technique. Some trainers do use punishment to stop unwanted behaviors, but a lot of them can be prevented by training the dog to do what you want him to do.

Punishment Disadvantages

Some trainers feel that punishment can be an effective tool for stopping unwanted behaviors if used correctly. However, to use punishment correctly, it must be done at the right time, with the right force, and for the right duration. The problem is that few dog trainers can use this powerful tool correctly, and there are numerous disadvantages to using it incorrectly.

One of the most common misuses of punishment is using it to correct a behavior rather than simply training the dog properly. For example, a dog who chases and nips at someone riding a bike isn't doing so to be bad but because he has a natural drive to chase—the action may bewilder the owner, but it makes perfect sense to the dog. The dog must be *trained* not to follow this natural urge, not punished when he does what comes naturally.

Another problem with punishment is that it is too often given in association with the wrong action. Take the dog who's chasing the bike—more than likely, the owner repeatedly calls the dog to come while the chase is going on. When the dog finally does return, he's punished in some way—by a jerk of the collar, a smack on the rump, or a scolding. In the owner's mind, the dog is being reprimanded for chasing that bike. The dog, however, connects the punishment with the last thing he did—coming when called. So, in essence, the dog was punished for returning to his owner when called. This kind of punishment, which attempts to stop an unwanted behavior, is more likely to teach the dog not to come when called than to convince him not to chase the bike.

Typically, for punishment to be effectively associated with the crime, it needs to come during the unwanted event or within seconds of drawing the dog's attention to the unwanted behavior. Otherwise, the dog is left guessing as to why and what the owner chose to punish. This is another reason why I don't recommend punishment.

Good body posture communicates that you are in charge.

General Training Rules

A lot of training involves communicating with your dog. Miscommunication can sabotage the results you want. Here are some rules to help you learn how to be more effective in your training.

Rule #1: Be Aware of Your Posture and Voice

One of the most valuable tools you use when training a dog is yourself. Dogs respond to more than a command—they pay attention to tone of voice and body language, which can be more valuable than any words you say. If you misuse these tools, you will confuse and frustrate your dog, or you could create an entirely different response than you want from him.

Your dog will respond to an assertive posture. Your head should be level, your back straight but not stiff, and your stance solid with your feet about shoulder length apart. This posture communicates to a dog that you're in charge. An assertive posture doesn't communicate any kind of harshness toward the dog but works to reassure him because you look more self-assured.

Tone of voice is also a useful tool. There are two kinds of voice tones that you can use to help train and control a dog. A high-pitched, happy, playful voice can be used to motivate a dog. A more self-assured voice, one that has even tones and deeper resonance, can be used to reassure a dog or to assert control.

Rule #2: Eliminate Distractions

Do your initial training in a quiet environment with as few distractions as possible. Once the dog understands what is expected, you can start working in an environment with more distractions.

Rule #3: Be Consistent With Your Commands

Clear, consistent commands make learning easier for a dog. Sometimes, two or more people in a family will want to work on training a dog. If this is the case, make sure that you use the same commands for a task. One of the more common misused commands is the *down*. If one person tells the dog "Down" when she wants the dog to lie down and another uses the same term to tell the dog to not jump up, the dog can become confused. It is better to give the "don't jump" command a different term, such as "off," so that the dog more immediately understands. However, this must be communicated to all members of the household, and everyone must be consistent with their terms. It's important

Training similar materials, like distinguishing between retrieving a right and left dumbbell, should be taught separately.

to work together as a team when practicing commands.

Rule #4: Make the Training Session the Right Length

The length of time you can train will vary with the dog's age and experience level. Young puppies have a very short attention span and must have brief lessons, as should highly distracted dogs and dogs with little tolerance for repetitive tasks. To lengthen training sessions with these dogs, gradually add a little more training time to each lesson. Also, breaking up training by playing in between the drilling can help lengthen the amount of time you can work the dog in one session.

Rule #5: Teach Similar Material Separately

Similar commands will need to be taught separately. Take a dumbbell retrieving exercise, for example—say that your dog needs to distinguish between retrieving a right and left dumbbell. Give a signal consistently for the right dumbbell until your dog masters it. Then switch to the left until he masters that direction. Don't expect to be able to train these tasks in the same day. Finally, mix the two commands, but don't drill your dog too long on the task. Also, don't go for subtle differences in commands. Later in the chapter, you'll find an example where a trainer used the word "go," which sounded too much like the word "no." This resulted in the dog becoming

When to Quit a Training Session

If a dog exhibits the following signs, it's time to end the training session.
- wandering attention
- sluggish response
- confusion
- whining, barking, or becoming fidgety
- shutting down, including lying down or walking away as if he was just scolded

upset and not doing a task that he'd been effectively trained to do. When you choose commands, do so with the idea that each command should be easy to distinguish.

Rule #6: Learn When to End a Lesson

Stop training long before the dog has had enough of the lesson—before he reaches his saturation point. While that point varies with each dog, the newer and more complex the material, the quicker the dog will reach a saturation point. Also, training that requires a dog to distinguish between two similar tasks (such as the dumbbell illustration mentioned earlier) can more quickly saturate a dog.

Trying to work a dog beyond his saturation point won't increase his learning and can create stress. Stress during training is destructive and can cause the dog to become resistant and reluctant to comply. (Punishment also causes stress—another

51

good reason not to use it.)

Quitting at a high point will help keep training positive and the dog's interest higher. With most dogs, quitting early, after you've had a success or two, can work faster than constant drilling.

Incorporate training into feeding time— before you set down your dog's food bowl, ask for a *sit*.

Rule # 7: Incorporate Training With Feeding

Because you have to feed your dog every day, don't hesitate to use this time to do a little training. Ask for a *sit* before you set down the food bowl, or toss a few pieces of kibble as a reward for doing one or two simple tasks. For a dog who is interested in your eating habits, instead of simply sharing your food, ask for a task. The dog can even practice a long *down-stay* while waiting for that tidbit from your supper table.

Rule #8: Timing Makes a Difference

Timing makes a difference with reinforcement. The closer to the action the reinforcement comes, the quicker the animal learns. That's why touching a hot stove is such an effective lesson—the pain comes almost simultaneously with touching the surface, leaving little guesswork as to why it hurt and how to prevent it from happening again. The quicker you give reinforcement, the quicker your dog figures out what you want him to do. When using negative reinforcement, if the reinforcer comes more than three seconds after the action, the dog is left guessing about what he did wrong.

Rule #9: Training Has a Correct Order

There is a right and wrong order when training. The order changes depending on whether you are doing initial training (first introducing a command), correcting a dog, or working to desensitize a dog. Doing your training in the wrong order can create training disasters.

The Correct Order for Teaching a New Command

When you are first teaching a new command, you can say the command word before *or* after the dog does what you want. For example, if you pick up a ball and your dog sits, you can say "Good sit" and reward

Desensitizing a dog has a correct order.

him by tossing the ball. Or you can pick up the ball, tell your dog to sit, and then toss the ball as a reward when he sits. Either order works fine when initially teaching a new command.

The Correct Order for Correcting a Behavior or Stopping an Action

There are times when you may find that you need to correct your dog's behavior or stop him from doing something. One popular word used to stop a dog from engaging in a particular action is the word "no." When giving a correction or teaching the word "no," give the command first, before you undertake any action to get the dog to abandon doing what you don't want him to do. By doing this in the right order, you allow him to choose to stop *before* you react to intervene. (Chapter 4 explains how to teach your dog the *no* command.)

The Correct Order for Desensitizing a Dog

If you are working to desensitize a dog, the order is extremely important. Sometimes dogs can become distressed or unnerved in new situations or as a result of loud noises. Many trainers will try to teach a dog to change his attitude by offering something positive (such as a reward or petting) to associate with the negative incident. The correct order is to offer the positive reinforcement *after* the negative incident has happened—never before. An example of how this works is in Chapter 9.

Sending Mixed Signals

Carol, an experienced dog trainer, practiced obedience with her German Shepherd Dog, Remus, for several months. During her first obedience competition, when she needed to send Remus off to fetch a dumbbell on the other side of a jump, she gave the command "Go." But Remus didn't do as he was trained; instead, he lay on the ground and began to shake.

Remus was showing distress because he was confused by Carol's command—he couldn't tell if Carol had said "Go" or "No." Although Carol had practiced the *go* command with Remus for months, he was getting mixed signals at the competition. When Carol practiced the *go* command during training she was relaxed, but during the competition, she was nervous. Remus sensed this negative energy—the same kind of negativity he associated with a reprimand like "No." Remus could not determine if Carol was reprimanding him or telling him to go and get the dumbbell. This precipitated a neurotic reaction in Remus, and he became upset, trembled, and could not continue in the competition.

Training Precautions

Good training techniques facilitate training; however, there are some training issues that people need to be aware of that can sabotage success.

Precaution #1: Don't Use Inconsistent Commands

Inconsistency in giving commands can create stress just as readily as punishment can. Dog owners who don't have a lot of training experience are often inconsistent with their commands. Earlier, we discussed an example in which some people use the word "down" to mean two different things.

First, "down" meant that the dog was supposed to lie down; later, it was used to tell the dog to get down, such as off a person or maybe a piece of furniture. You will find a lot of suggestions for verbal commands in this book. Although you can use any word to teach your dog any action, you may want to make a list as you read and decide what words work best for you.

Once you choose your list of commands, mentally rehearse them when you aren't training. Say the command, and then practice acknowledging that response quickly. When correcting, give the command first, then work with your dog to get the right response. When initially teaching him, you can give the command after he has offered a desired behavior. This can increase your awareness and polish with giving commands, help you give them in the right order, and help with your timing of acknowledging the dog's correct response, which facilitates learning. If you find that you are having difficulty with training, sometimes finding a training coach can help you learn to give commands, acknowledgments, and rewards in the correct order and with good timing.

Precaution #2: Don't Use Commands That Are too Similar

Using commands that have subtle differences can create extreme stress for a dog, like confusing *go* and *no*. (See box on page 54.) One of Ivan Pavlov's canine behavior experiments demonstrated this effect. He tried ringing a bell and giving a reward of meat powder, then ringing a bell with a completely different tone and giving no reward. The dogs quickly learned which bell signaled a reward and which one didn't, leaving the dogs quite content. However,

Don't use inconsistent commands or you could create stress in your dog.

Eye Contact

If you are looking at your dog and thinking angry thoughts, you may be giving him what can be interpreted as a dominant eye stare. Never ask a dog to look at you when you are mad or try to force a stare into your dog's eyes. This goes strongly against his culture.

when Pavlov changed the tone of the bell that didn't give a reward to almost the same tone as the bell that did give a reward, the dogs became neurotic because they could not distinguish between the two tones.

If a dog suddenly seems to want to quit in the middle of a lesson, or if he becomes agitated or stressed, he may be suffering from training stresses that can precipitate a neurosis. Some of the signs include agitation, barking, or whining; some agitated dogs may even snap, growl, or become sullen. If you see these issues when training, stop what you are doing and examine your techniques. Be sure that your cues are clear and unique from other commands.

Precaution #3: Don't Give an Unintended Visual Signal

It isn't unusual for people to give one cue verbally and then contradict that cue with an unintended visual signal. Agility competitors run into this problem all the time. The dog handler may call out a jump and even flip a hand in that direction, only to have the dog go through a tunnel. What

the handler didn't realize was that her feet were pointing toward the tunnel, and the dog followed that cue over the verbal cue.

Consistency means handling all cues well. If you are having a problem, seek the help of a dog professional who is good at reading unintended cues to help you learn consistency.

Precaution #4: Don't Use Improper Training Tools

Training techniques like a harsh eye stare, alpha roll, or scruff shake are strongly discouraged for use with any dog.

Dominant Eye Stare

Dogs do a lot of communicating with their eyes. In the next chapter, you will learn how to use eye contact as a powerful tool. However, using eye contact incorrectly can cause problems. A harsh and direct stare (or dominant eye stare) is a challenge used by a dog who is in power.

The dog receiving the eye stare can choose to look away or meet that challenge with a fight.

Some trainers deliberately use a dominance-related eye stare on problematic dogs to assert authority over the dog. However, this technique can cause some dogs to become overly submissive, while others may decide that they need to aggressively take the defense. Using this technique can solicit a bite from a dog, and because few people understand the subtle rules about using this method correctly, I don't recommend it.

Alpha Rolls

Alpha rolls can have the same consequences as dominant eye stares. The technique was derived directly from alpha dogs who forcibly roll a subordinate dog onto his back. I've seen an alpha dog roll over and pin a subordinate dog, then give the subordinate a threatening growl. The subordinate dog got the message that the alpha dog was not to be challenged. However, dogs are much better at knowing when and how to use this technique than people are.

Dogs have subtle cues and nonverbal messages they can read off each other that most people miss. Like the dominance-related eye stare, alpha rolls should be left in the hands of canines and not used by dog owners. Although these techniques are used by some dog trainers, they are not easy to use correctly, and incorrect use can have grave consequences.

Scruff Shake

Some dog owners find it easy to pick up a smaller dog by the scruff of his neck. However, this can communicate unwanted messages to your dog. An alpha dog will sometimes discipline a subordinate dog by grabbing his neck scruff and shaking. By imitating this action, you are putting your dog into a submissive position. Some dogs don't need to become more submissive, and others may fight you for trying to put them in this submissive position. Even dogs who don't react adversely are being needlessly dominated. Although a dog who trusts and respects you may tolerate being picked up by the scruff, it isn't recommended.

Do not use improper training tools like alpha rolls or scruff shakes.

Basic and Advanced Training

Part Two

Chapter Four

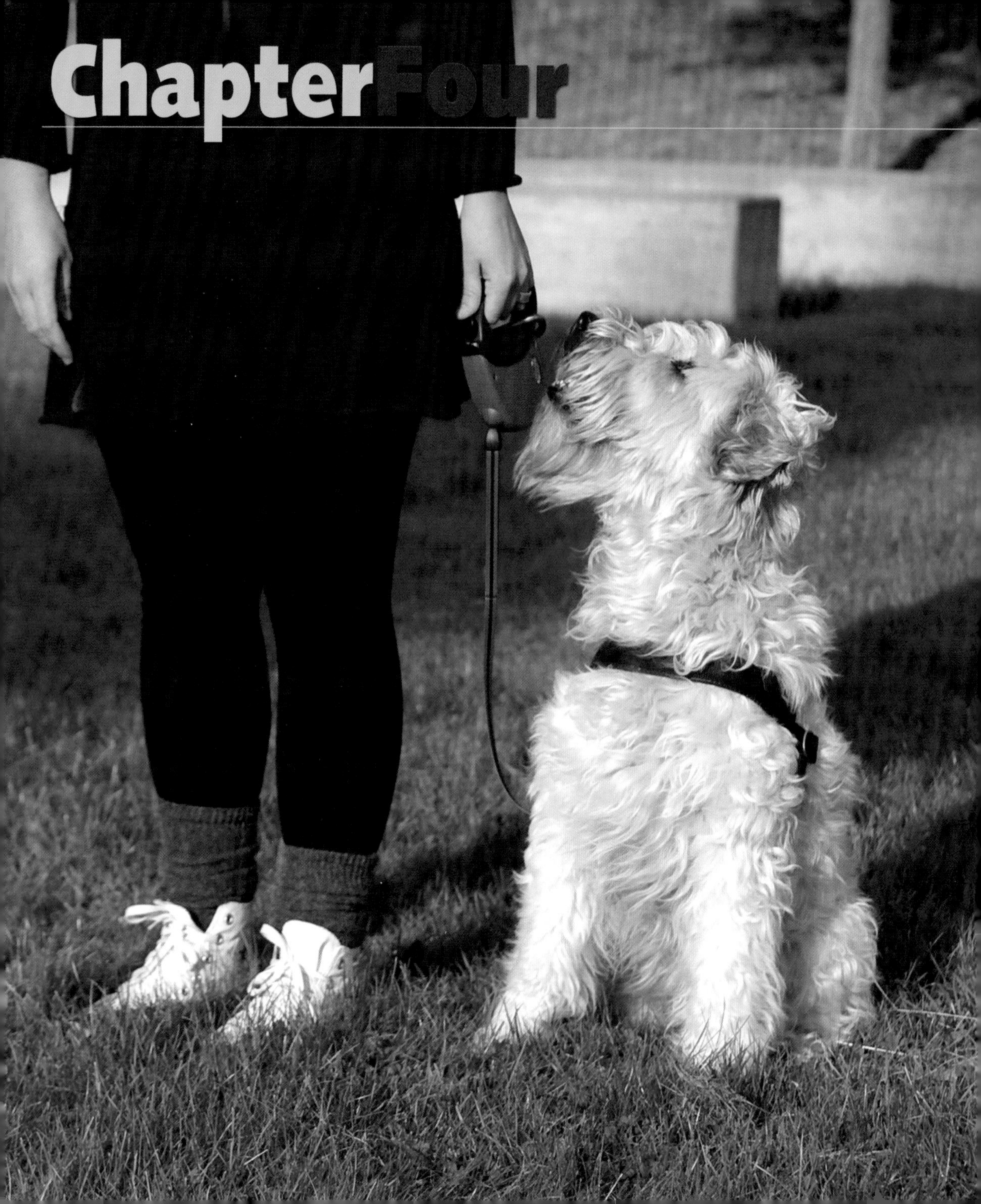

Teaching theBasics

Teaching basics like *sit*, *down*, and *stay* may seem unimportant when what you really want is for your dog to stop chasing the cat or not snap at you when you try to take away his toy. However, basic training has hidden advantages. It creates a foundation to build on, which allows you to regain control of an out-of-control dog. Basic training can also help you hone your training skills and develop a relationship with your dog. The better you are at giving good, solid cues, the easier it will be when working to reform unwanted behaviors. Plus, the better your relationship with your dog—especially one built on him obeying a command—the more overall control you will have.

Training Has Evolved

As mentioned in Chapter 3, after World War II, the popular way to train a dog equated to doing a lot of yanking on a choke collar and punishing any misbehaviors. Then the trend for positive techniques began, and many trainers reassessed their skills and found that by training commands using positive reinforcement (as in the basic training discussed in this chapter), they didn't have to resort to yanking or jerking on the leash. Positive training removes the need to correct a dog and is by far the best way to train him.

I am a strong supporter of positive training and have taught classes to help educate people on how to train their dogs in this manner. Although it takes time to hone your skills to train well, the effort is worthwhile, especially considering that most people plan to have more than one dog in their lives. However, over the years, I have discovered that some people can't or won't acquire the skills for this superior training—and they have problematic dogs whose issues must be resolved to prevent them from being given up. For those reasons, I do occasionally believe that corrections are necessary. While it may go against the current training trends, I feel that as long as the corrections are not harsh and are done properly, they can help reform a hard-to-train dog. Wherever possible, though, I strive to keep my training suggestions as positive as I can while still helping less-skilled owners obtain results with their difficult dogs.

Training Tools

To teach the basic commands, you'll need the following tools.

Leash

You'll need a 4- to 6-foot (1- to 2-m) leash. Nylon is fine, but if you find that your dog chews on it, you may want to use a lightweight chain leash. You may need to use a drag leash, which is a long, lightweight leash used for distance training.

Collar

A regular or wide collar works best, typically 3/4 to 1 inch (2 to 2.5 cm). I often use a nylon collar, but a leather one is also fine.

Choke or Slip Collars

Choke collars come in two varieties: chain and nylon. Both have rings on each end of the material. The collar can be adjusted so that it will tighten when pulled. Many trainers still recommend the use of these devices—jerking them for a correction or pulling them tight to try to influence a dog. The choking they create is also used to discourage a dog from pulling. However, these types of collars can destroy a dog's throat. Autopsies performed on dogs trained with a choke collar have revealed severe damage to their tracheas. For some dogs, using these devices for even a short period will result in irreparable damage. Because of the possible damage to a dog's throat, I do not recommend choke or slip collars.

Pinch or Prong Collars

The pinch (or prong) collar is a modified form of the choke collar. It tightens and releases in a similar manner as a choke collar; however, prongs discourage the dog from pulling against the device and so prevent throat damage. Although this device looks cruel, the pinch collar is better for most dogs than a choke collar because it doesn't damage

These types of choke and prong collars are not recommended.

Using a Leash as a Tool for Training

Years ago, in an obedience class, I learned a poor way to use a leash for training. The instructor had us fit our dogs with a choke chain collar and give a jerk every time the dog needed to be corrected—for example, if the dog walked too far ahead instead of heeling. Since then, I have found better ways to use a leash for training. With a regular collar or a martingale harness, such as the Easy Walker Training Aid, I use the leash to communicate with a dog. I can guide him using the leash and help him understand what I want. Sometimes I pull on the leash to stop forward motion, while other times I will give a gentle tug if I need to reclaim the dog's attention. However, I don't use constant jerks on a leash. It's unnecessary, and many dogs often end up ignoring them anyway.

the throat. However, the collar still has drawbacks. Some dogs respond poorly with this collar, increasing aggression toward other dogs. I do not recommend pinch collars unless under specific guidance from a professional.

Treats

Treats are often used for reward-based training. The size of the treat shouldn't be large—small pieces can motivate while keeping the dog from becoming full or overfed. Many dog biscuits can be broken into pieces, and some dog foods come in

Alexis and the Choke Collar

Years ago, my daughter's Jack Russell Terrier, Alexis, went to a puppy class to help socialize her. The class instructor believed in using a choke chain collar when teaching a dog to heel, as was common at the time. Alexis was a star pupil when it came to heeling, much to the instructor's amazement—the teacher noted "Jack Russells don't heel, especially at this age. I just don't get it." What the instructor didn't know was that my daughter had begun to study positive techniques and was using rewards instead of leash corrections, creating a better-behaved dog.

Because choke collars were highly recommended by so many trainers, we continued to use this device for the next year, along with the rewards method. Although Alexis heeled most of the time when out on walks, if she saw a squirrel ahead of her, she'd go into pulling mode. In no time at all, Alexis began to cough excessively right after the choke collar made contact. Her throat had quickly become damaged by the choke collar, even though, she didn't pull excessively compared to many dogs. We tried a very wide collar on her, but the damage had already been done, and even slight pressure for occasional pulls would send her into coughing fits.

Next, we tried a regular harness, but sometimes it would slip up to her throat and cause the same issues. A regular harness, where the leash attaches in between the dog's shoulder blades, does not discourage pulling.

We then tried a Gentle Leader (harness). Like many dogs, Alexis didn't like this device a lot, but it did keep her throat safe. We switched to a Halti (head halter), which Alexis objected to less. Finally, after the Gentle Walker harness came out, we gave that a try. It kept Alexis from pulling and never bothered her throat.

After seeing the damage a choke collar can cause, I am extremely opposed to ever using this kind of device. After talking with other trainers, I have heard of a few instances where choke collars have actually done enough damage to kill a dog.

small chunks. Even tiny pieces of cheese or meat can be a motivating reward. A good-sized treat is easy to handle and can be eaten in one chomp rather than the dog needing to stop and chew it up.

Good Treats

- Regular dog food or kibble. Sometimes your dog may prefer a different brand than your regular dog food as a nice variety.

- Small chunks of meat or cheese.
- Soft dog biscuits.

Bad Treats
- Chocolate and raisins, which are toxic to dogs.
- Onions and similar foods, including garlic and onion salt, which can cause anemia.
- Fatty foods, including chicken skin, pork fat, and fatty ham trimmings, which can trigger pancreatic problems in some dogs.

Using Rewards

Years ago, a second-generation dog trainer who specialized in training bird dogs for hunting shared his core philosophy with me. He said that there is a great advantage when training if you can arrange to provide a dog with solutions rather than dish out punishment. His philosophy meant that by working *with* a dog, you could become a team. Training with rewards can allow you and your dog to become a team.

By using positive training techniques, you teach your dog that there is a reward for compliance, allowing you to become part of the solution and not the problem. If your dog desires a treat, all he needs to do is follow your request and you'll be there with a tasty reward when he completes the task. By allowing your dog to choose compliance and not forcing it upon him, you're taking a

Many dogs find treats very rewarding, which can be used in their training.

Never Free Feed a Dog

One way to sabotage treat training is to free feed a dog, a method in which food is left out all day for him to eat whenever he wants. A dog who is continually fed will have less interest in earning a treat and may not find treats motivating at all. However, beware of the dog who is too hungry—he may become so excited about getting something into his tummy that he will struggle to focus on what you want him to learn.

leadership role and forming a valuable bond with him. With the correct use of reward-based training, such as treats, you're not bribing your dog into compliance—instead, you're using them as a reward to help create the habit of compliance.

Treats Need to Be Varied and Faded

Feeding the same treat over and over works for a dog who is highly food motivated. However, some dogs may quickly lose interest in the same old dog biscuit. To prevent this problem, mix up the kinds of treats you use. Save some of the best-tasting rewards when you need to give your dog extra motivation.

When your dog is learning a new task, give him treats consistently. Over time, fade the food reward, which means that you should gradually eliminate it. To do this, start giving the reward every other time, then every third time, and finally only once in a while. When fading a treat, offer praise and petting as a substitute (especially because they are rewards you can always carry with you!). However, you may find that highly distracted or low-motivated dogs and dogs who don't cherish praise as a reward need more frequent food rewards.

What Is a "Jackpot"?

What if your boss said that you were getting a big raise? You'd probably be really happy. What if the next year your boss said, "Wasn't it great, that big raise I gave you last year? You're getting the same this year"? Okay, getting any raise is nice, but the excitement would be gone. What if your boss then said, "You're getting the same raise as last year. And because I'm so happy with your work, I'm giving you an extra monetary bonus right now"? You'd be back to being excited and enthused because you had that extra-special bonus to enjoy.

In training terms, that extra bonus is a "jackpot," or a higher-value reward. During training sessions, rewarding with treats is typical. But if your dog finally does a task *exactly* the way you want, you can reward him with a jackpot. Create a jackpot by giving several treats instead of one or by using something the dog likes better than the usual reward.

Play Training

Not all dogs are food motivated. For some, play is more rewarding than a treat, and this tends to be the case with high-drive and overly assertive dogs. Play training can be used with any dog who has lost interest in a task or who doesn't seem to have a lot of interest in treats.

To use play in training, hold out a toy as if it were a treat and then ask your dog to do a command. The instant he does what you ask, say "Yes" in an excited voice and begin to play with the toy.

Controlling the Play

Some dogs may become too excited when playing to pay attention to the lesson. If this happens, try switching the kind of toy

For some dogs, using play is more rewarding than a treat.

you use. If your dog gets too hyper with a squeak toy, try using one that doesn't make noise. If fur gets your dog too wild, try a plastic toy. Put away the toys when you aren't using them for playing or training. By controlling the toys, you can teach your dog that the best way to get playtime is through compliance.

Getting Started

You should teach your dog marker words like "good" and "yes," and teach him a release word to indicate when the task is finished.

"Yes" and "Good"

Good timing is essential for training. Unfortunately, it takes time to get a treat to your dog's mouth when he does something right. To let him know the instant he does what you want, you can use a word to acknowledge the exact moment that he does so. Trainers call this marking desired behavior, which means that you're acknowledging the event the instant it happens. For every second that passes that you don't let your dog know he did something right, there is less of a chance that he will associate the correct response with the reward. Sometimes, by the time you're able to hand over the treat, your dog is involved in another behavior—and it may not be one you want to encourage. To solve this problem, teach your dog the words "yes" and "good," which will help mark the correct behavior. Here's how to teach your dog to associate both words with a reward.

Useful Commands With Play Training

During play training, some dogs get so intense about playing that it's helpful to teach a command to let them know that this small bit of reward playing is over. A good command to use is *all done* or just *done*. This is not the same as a release word, which means that a command is no longer being asked for. This is a word to end an action that the dog might want to continue, which is your option to enforce because you are the leader. Likewise, you will probably need to teach your dog to let go of the toy. This is where the *give* command comes in handy. (See Chapter 5.)

did the task right. This will help him learn more quickly what action he needs to take to secure a reward.

Release Word

Release words let your dog know that he no longer has to respond to a command. Technically, if you tell your dog to sit, he should sit until you tell him to stop. To communicate that the exercise is over, you can teach him a release word like "okay," "all done," or "release."

To teach this command, say "Okay," then walk away as if you no longer have any interest in the event. Most dogs pick up that this means that the task is over. If your dog doesn't abandon the task after a few moments, give another command, such as "Come," and reward that task.

Basic Commands

Basic obedience training is one of the easiest ways to begin to take a leadership role with your dog. Following are some of the basic commands and some troubleshooting tips for the hard-to-train dog.

Sit

One command I find very useful is the *sit* command. I can use this to do other training with a dog, such as teaching him to make eye contact. Also, by putting him into a *sit*, I can better get him to give me his attention.

To teach this command, use a treat to lure your dog into a sitting position.

1. Feed him several treats in a row while saying "Good" or "Yes" each time.
2. Don't hesitate to praise and pet your dog while he's munching away on the treat.
3. Both commands can be taught in the same training session without confusing your dog.

Typically, it is best to use "good" when your dog is on the right track of completing a task (when you are shaping the behavior) and "yes" to let him know that the task is done or that the end point is reached. Although feeding the treat is the real reward, by using the word "yes," you can get your dog to realize the exact moment he

1. Show your dog the treat, then pull it

backward over his head, making sure that you don't go faster than your dog can track the treat.

2. A dog will usually lower his back end while trying to get the treat.
3. Say "Good" any time your dog's back end gets closer to the ground.
4. The instant your dog sits, say "Yes" and reward.

As discussed in the previous chapter, you can choose to teach the command first, and then after the dog starts offering the action, you can attach a command word. Or you can say the word and use a treat to lure your dog into the action. The moment he performs the action, you can use your praise word to mark exactly when the command was correctly accomplished.

If you find that your dog doesn't want to comply with your request, you may need to take him to a less distracting environment. Also, sometimes offering a treat for free will get him to better focus on you; then you can use a second treat to lure him into a *sit*.

If He Won't Sit

Dogs who show excess resistance to learning how to sit may have compliance

Lure your dog into the *sit* position with a treat, and reward.

issues. You need to solve the compliance resistance before proceeding to any other training. In other words, you must find a way to gain your dog's cooperation.

If your dog is showing indifference to food rewards, train before dinnertime and use very tasty treats. Give him the first treat without any commands to get his attention and to interest him in your reward. Then work to get at least one *sit* by luring with a single treat. After one *sit*, praise excessively and continue the praise while you set down the food dish. Each night, only request one *sit* for his food dish until you notice him himself. ... anticipation ... cern yourself if this ... ek or two. You don't have a ... er—you have a dog who needs to ... the value of cooperation.

Once your dog begins to offer the *sit* before you ask for it, say "Good sit" and give him the treat but not the bowl of food. Instead, pick up the food dish and take a couple steps away until your dog abandons his *sit*. As soon as he gets up, ask him to sit. When he does, put down the food dish. Slowly work up to three or four *sits* (rewarding each one with a small bite), and then give the entire meal for that last *sit*. Watch for his attitude to change from reluctance about sitting on command to willingness to earn that treat. When your dog's attitude changes, you are ready to move on in your training.

Wouldn't It Be Easier to Push Down the Dog's Rump and Tell Him to Sit?

It's better to build cooperation with a dog than to force him to do a command, and this is especially true with stubborn, strong-willed, and assertive dogs. Using positive techniques and letting the dog choose to comply are better choices.

If He Refuses to Lure With Any Treat

Just as some dogs come hardwired to please, some seem to have a predisposition to resist commands—until you prove to them that compliance is a good thing. Your dog may sit to earn the bowl of food, but the next time, for no apparent reason, he may decide not to comply. If this happens, you'll have to work a bit harder to show your dog that there is a reward in compliance. Getting a *sit* is no longer the goal, so don't try to push his back end down and force the issue. The real goal is to get him to decide to sit because he realizes that following your commands is not a big deal and in fact can be a good thing.

If you find that you have a dog who doesn't want to lure with a treat, change your tactic to rewarding the behavior before you ask for it. Start by hiding several of your dog's favorite treats inside your pocket so that he can't see the reward. You may want to put the treats in a plastic bag to help cover up any smell. Once those treats are secure, follow your dog around the house. When he happens to sit, quickly say "Sit" and then toss the treat. After he eats the treat, if he decides to jump all over you to demand another morsel, turn your back on him but peek over your shoulder. With some dogs, you may need to keep turning your back several times until he gives up. If your dog happens to sit again at any point, even if your back is to him, say "Sit" and reward. Watch for your dog to begin offering the behavior so that he can get rewards. You're convincing him that he has something to gain by learning to follow your command. Once you conquer his resistance to the *sit*, you can launch into more training. Teaching your dog that it is in his best interest to learn to comply with a command will make further training much easier.

Down

Down can be a useful command for a few reasons. If you are waiting at a veterinary office, it is nice to have a dog who lies peacefully by your feet. The *down* position is also one that a dog assumes when he is comfortable with his owner's authority. Dogs who learn to down also learn to relinquish control to their owners.

To teach *down*:

1. Ask your dog to sit.
2. Show him a treat.
3. Say the word "down," then use the treat to lure his front end downward.
4. He may not drop all the way to the floor with the first try; however, if he gets a reward each time he gets a little lower, he will eventually make it all the way down.
5. When your dog reaches his final goal, say "Yes" and award a jackpot.

Using "Good" and "Yes" With Down

The *down* is a good place to illustrate the use of "good" and "yes." Let's say that you lure with the treat and the front end of your dog goes down, but the back end is still up.

A Hard Compliance Case

Many people fell in love with the well-trained Jack Russell Terrier, Moose, who played Eddie on the TV series *Frasier*. Moose was given away by his original owners because they could not get him to follow any commands. He had not only taken charge, he'd learned that doing so was rewarding. Moose had a lot of fun misbehaving, and he seemed to have decided that treats weren't as important to him as being his "own dog." He had very little interest in luring to sit even for a treat.

Moose was adopted by a trainer who began his reform by finding a way to teach him that there was a reward for compliance. To start, Moose's trainer rewarded an action that the dog did naturally, then attached a command to it. The final step was to only reward the dog when the command was followed.

Moose loved to jump and would do it quite readily on his own, so his trainer started there. She took a treat and held it over Moose's head. When he jumped for the treat, she immediately gave the *jump* command, then gave the reward. After Moose got the idea that a jump received a reward, she used the command first and then presented the treat. Soon, Moose learned that if he jumped on command, he got a treat. This launched into more training with treats as a reward. By beginning with a behavior the dog already offered, Moose's trainer turned a misbehaved dog into a star performer.

Down can be a useful command because it teaches your dog to lie peacefully at your feet.

Use the word "good" to tell your dog that he's on the right track and needs to continue to get to the place that earns his reward. Each time your dog lowers his back end a little, say "Good." Now let's say that your dog finally plops down his back end—here's where you want to say "Yes" and reward with a treat.

If He Won't Down

Some dogs seem to have a hard time getting into the *down* position. At times it can help to lightly put your hand on your dog's back. Don't push—just make contact with his back. This action can make a dog want to move away from what feels like a barrier and help him drop to the floor.

Come (Recall)

There are many ways to teach *come*, and the variety is needed for good reasons. It's a difficult command to master, and oftentimes you must tailor the training to your dog's individual needs. Although the methods listed in this section certainly don't describe every possible way to teach *come*, they will work for most dogs. Make sure that your dog is willing to comply with the other basic commands before you teach *come* because this command is one that some dogs may resist following.

Training a Puppy to Come

As mentioned previously, puppies are dependent learners. If you are fortunate enough to begin training in the puppy stage, you can take advantage of your puppy's willingness to follow a leader and build a good foundation for compliance.

To teach a puppy to come, use a higher-pitched voice, which will make him more willing to follow. You can also clap your hands when you say "Come." By using a more excited voice or by clapping your hands, you'll get your puppy's attention. Be willing to take a few steps away after you say "Come," and keep encouraging your puppy to come to you with these signals. Reward him when he comes.

Training an Adolescent to Come

As an adolescent dog experiments with his independence, he will often ignore the *come* command. In fact, you may find that your willing puppy is no longer willing to come when called once he reaches adolescence. For this reason, I strongly recommend using a leash to enforce the command. Sometime

Never Call a Dog for Punishment

Punishing your dog is never a good idea, and you never want to call him to you to punish misbehavior. Stopping the unwanted behavior by calling your dog to come must suffice until you find a way to train for the behavior you want. When you punish your dog after calling him over to you, you are actually punishing him for coming and not for the unwanted behavior.

a retractable leash can be used. Let your dog wander out but not to the point where he pulls on the leash. Call him to come, and if he doesn't, use the leash to guide him back to you. Praise him when he arrives, and give him a treat. I like to make it a point to continually reward a dog when he comes on command during adolescence to help develop a more secure response. When your dog learns to come in response to your command and doesn't need to be directed with the leash, you are ready to let him off leash (in an enclosed space) and try a *recall*. But don't rush this process. Some adolescent dogs may comply one day or for one week and not the next. Typically, I prefer to wait to let a dog off leash until after he is a year old.

Training an Adult to Come

Adults can be taught in a fashion similar to that used for adolescents. You can also take an adult to an enclosed field and practice coming using a long drag leash. Reward with treats when your dog comes. Also, do your *recall* several times before leaving the field so that your dog doesn't think that coming always means that the fun he is having is going to end. (Pick up any dog messes in this area before you leave.)

If He Won't Come

Too many people create problems with the *come* command by not fully understanding how it should be trained. They end up with an unreliable *recall* or sometimes even "untrain" the dog by calling for the wrong reasons.

First, don't call your dog to come for anything unpleasant. If you call him to come when you plan to clip his nails, punish him, or do anything he won't like, you are in essence sabotaging the *come* command. You are giving him reasons not to want to come to you.

Second, if your dog has a reliable *recall* in your backyard, this does not mean that he will be reliable out in a park or some other new area. To learn to come reliably, dogs need to be trained in areas with lots of distractions. This training can be done by using a long lead or retractable leash, and always remember to reward your dog when he arrives. Once he consistently chooses to return without needing help, he can be let off leash.

The best way to keep your dog coming to you is to always keep his compliance to the command positive. Don't hesitate to give praise or rewards on occasion, even after he has been trained.

Always reward your dog for coming when called—never punish him.

How Hard Is a Tug?

A leash should be used in a friendly manner. Think of how a friend might put her hand on your shoulder to get your attention or redirect what you are doing. This is ideally how a leash should be used when trying to redirect your dog or get his attention. Depending on your dog and his level of distraction, how lightly you can effectively handle your leash will vary.

Two Important Command Words: "No" and "Watch"

Teaching the *no* and *watch* commands will help establish your leadership and control of your dog.

The No Command

Some dogs pick up that the word "no" means to stop doing something merely by the tone of the word. Other dogs may need to be taught what the word "no" means or may understand the word but decide that the misbehavior is too rewarding and not want to stop. In these kinds of situations, you must enforce the word "no." Although this was discussed somewhat in the previous chapter, here are some more ways to work on teaching the *no* command.

1. Attach a leash to your dog.
2. If he does something you want him to stop, say "No."
3. If he doesn't stop, use gentle tug on the leash to get his attention and stop him from completing the unwanted action.
4. Next, call your dog over to you and have him sit in front of you.
5. When he sits, give a treat and some praise as a reward.
6. After you've rewarded your dog, release him from the *sit* and turn away, but don't let go of that leash.
7. If he takes up the unwanted behavior again, repeat the previous steps, telling him "No" and using the leash to stop him.
8. Once again, redirect your dog to sit in front of you, then reward and praise.
9. After releasing him, see if he repeats the misbehavior.
10. If so, repeat the steps again, but after your dog sits and is praised, walk away from the situation.

Basically, you are limiting this action to three times, then removing your dog from the situation. By repeating the steps three times, you will communicate to your dog that he is to stop when you say "No."

Proofing Your Training

A lot of failures with the basic commands happen because people don't train in a more distracting environment. Many dogs will perform a command if there is nothing else they want to do, but when offered a distraction, suddenly they won't comply. Training a dog in places and situations that tempt him to pursue his own desires is called proof training. It's a good idea to take your dog to more distracting places and work on your commands. Just make sure that he is securely on a leash.

If He Won't Listen to "No"

Some dogs will not change until they've had a chance to think about the behavior and consciously decide to comply. If you own this kind of dog, you may need to repeat a training session like the one just described several times. The next day is often a good time to see if your dog is now willing to comply with your *no* command. Keep up the schedule of three corrections a day, followed by a redirection and a reward, until he stops the behavior. Several training sessions may be in order, making this training seem tedious. However, this type of training builds on itself, and the next time you ask your dog to give up an unwanted behavior, he'll learn to comply sooner.

The Perils of Letting "No" Lose Its Meaning

For the *no* command to have significance to your dog, he not only needs to understand the negative content of the word, but you need to enforce its use. If you tell your dog "No" and he stops the action but immediately starts up again, or if he fails to stop when told "No," then your dog has lost the meaning of the word.

This kind of behavior often starts as a test. Your dog wants to know if you are willing to follow through with a command. A good leader will follow through, and a weak leader won't. Many dog owners lose control because they don't follow though with compliance, which makes them poor leaders in their dogs' eyes. This leads to some dogs picking and choosing which commands they will follow. This is part of a dog's inherited pack rules: Poor leaders don't deserve to be followed.

If you find that your dog decides not to comply, allowing this noncompliance to continue will work against your leadership status. You don't need to micromanage your dog's behavior, but if he decides to do things his way once, watch for a repeat of this behavior because you can't allow noncompliance to continue. If your dog shows noncompliance a second time, take action to make him comply. If you find that your dog is not stopping a behavior when you tell him "No," you don't need to punish him, but you do need to stop him from continuing the unwanted behavior.

The Watch Command—A True Powerhouse of Training

Teaching your dog the *watch* command trains him on several levels at once. By training him to look at you, he will learn to see you as a leader. Also, the *watch* command teaches your dog to pay attention to you, and when he's focused on you, he won't be engaging in an unwanted behavior, and he won't miss a command you are giving him.

I break the *watch* command into two lessons. With some dogs, the first lesson and a few practices afterward may be enough to teach the command. However, after working with so many dogs who are resistant about following commands, I've learned that breaking up the lesson into two parts can be helpful. If you are having control problems with your dog, trying to accomplish this command in one lesson may not work. So be prepared to ask for a little control the first time, and make sure that your dog realizes that there is a reward for this action. By taking control a little at a time, you are more likely to win his compliance.

"No" Can Be Overused

Too often, people use the word "no" for too many things, leaving their dogs guessing what their owners *really* want. For example, say your dog is happily eating a piece of trash he found in the road. Saying the word "no" may not communicate to him that he needs to drop that half-rotted hamburger someone chucked out the car window. He may be thinking that the word "no" means that you're going to come running toward him in yet another unwarranted bad mood, so he had better finish eating quickly or run off if he wants to keep eating. A better command in this case is *drop it*, which communicates to your dog to drop whatever he has in his mouth. (Learn how to train *drop it* in Chapter 5.)

Lesson One

1. Ask your dog to sit.
2. Next, hold a treat out sideways by stretching out your arm.
3. Typically, your dog will stare at the treat, especially if he thinks that doing so will get him that reward.
4. Wait for him to break his stare at the treat. (It may take up to five minutes.)
5. The instant he breaks the stare, immediately say "Yes" and toss the treat as a reward.
6. Repeat this process of holding out the treat and waiting.

7. Typically, a dog will again stare at the treat but will glance away from the treat a little sooner.
8. Be ready to acknowledge your dog making the choice to look away from the treat—say "Yes," and reward as soon as he does.

You are teaching your dog that he needs to do something other than stare at the treat to get a reward. Some dogs will move along quicker with this lesson than others. Be

Training the *watch* command will help your dog see you as a leader.

77

patient, and realize that with each lesson, things will improve. Even with a dog who takes a long time to conform, the results are well worth the effort. Keep in mind that your dog is not just learning to look at you for a treat—he is submitting to you with this action. He must relinquish control to you to get a reward.

With the first lesson, at the very least you should get your dog to look away from the treat two or three times. Some dogs are quicker to give up the power of staring at what they want and may even make eye contact with you by the end of the first lesson. If your dog is hesitant, you may have a bigger issue with compliance than you realized. Taking the time to get your dog to comply with this task will make a difference in later training.

Lesson Two

Sometimes you may be able to move on to the second lesson after several hours have passed from the first lesson, or the next day. However, if you find that your dog is extremely resistant to the *watch* command, repeat the first lesson until he stops resisting. Once he is more willing to give you a glance, you are ready to move on to the second lesson.

In the second lesson, a dog who is willing to comply with this command will often decide to quickly give you the response you want. Be ready to reward with that treat. However, there are some dogs who may persist in staring at the treat as if they learned nothing in the first lesson.

Even with a dog who takes a long time to conform to the *watch* command, the results are well worth the effort.

A stronger-willed dog may value doing things his way so much that he'll try to get you to hand over the treat on his terms. Likewise, a more assertive breed may want to outsmart you on this issue. With these kinds of dogs, the second session may be less successful than the first, but be persistent. This lesson is one of the best ways to plant some strong seeds in stubborn dogs, which can grow deep roots toward compliance.

1. Begin with the treat in your outstretched arm as you did in lesson one; most dogs will start to look away from the treat more quickly than they did in lesson one.
2. Continue to acknowledge the first glance away from the treat with a "Yes," followed by rewarding with the treat.
3. After two or three rewards, when your dog glances away from the treat, instead of saying "Yes" say "Good," but don't reward the good command with a treat.
4. Some dogs will stare elsewhere and not look at you for a long time. If your dog goes from that blank stare at nothing and turns his head a little your way, say "Yes" and reward with a treat.
5. After he has received a few reinforcements for looking toward you, the next time he glances toward you, tell him "Good," but don't reward with a treat.
6. At this point, your dog may glance at you as if he is wondering why you're not tossing the treat.
7. When you get that first glance into your eyes, even though it may be brief, say "Yes" and reward him with a jackpot of treats and some praise.
8. The second time he looks into your eyes, award another jackpot but one not quite as big.

If your dog was slow to accomplish this much eye contact, end the lesson here. If, however, he seems interested in doing what it takes to get that treat, continue to the next part immediately instead later or the next day as part of a new training session.

1. After a few successful eye contacts, withhold the treat until your dog makes more solid eye contact.
2. Slowly work on longer and longer eye contact by hesitating before acknowledging with your "Good." When you tell your dog "Good," don't give a treat, but use the word as encouragement. At this point, you will be asking for more before you award a treat.
3. If your dog is looking right back at the treat as soon as he gets a "Good" from you for a brief glance, you will

Another Technique to Train Eye Contact

A trainer named Janice Dearth had a very good technique to encourage eye contact. For a couple weeks, she'd carry around small, human-edible treats in her pocket. She'd put a treat in her mouth, and every time the dog glanced at her, she'd spit the treat. This method can help reform a less cooperative dog by focusing on what he has to gain when he cooperates rather than on what he fears he will lose by getting a reward on your terms.

Roxie Shows Her Stubborn Streak

Roxie is an almost pure white Jack Russell Terrier. As an assertive dog, Roxie quickly found ways to take charge of her household. She decided which commands she'd comply with, especially the *come* command. To begin Roxie's reform, I instructed her owner, Leslie, to teach her the *watch* command using the directions listed in this chapter. I knew that Leslie was giving clear commands and Roxie understood what she needed to do to get the reward. However, Roxie was not yet ready to comply.

At first, Roxie would glance at Leslie to get the treat, but then Roxie decided to take control—just like she had in other situations. She began to refuse to look toward Leslie and would persist in staring at the treat. Leslie countered this action by holding out the treat and not giving in. Leslie reported that for almost a week, Roxie seemed to barely be able to turn her head, as if her neck muscles were too stiff to move. Leslie said that it was almost comical to watch her dog struggle not to give in, and she was only able to ask for compliance once or twice a training session. However, persistence did pay off, and Roxie eventually gave up the power battle, performing the *watch* command whenever Leslie asked. Making sure that Roxie complied with this training became important in working to reform some of her other compliance issues.

need to ask for at least three glances at you before you treat. Given time, your dog will begin to stare longer the first time. Once a longer stare is achieved, you can reward and work toward even longer stares. Don't forget to encourage each short glance with the word "good;" then with the third glance, you can say "Yes" and reward.

4. Soon your dog will stop glancing away and hold a longer eye contact.

Don't practice too long in each lesson. A few eye contacts are great. If your dog finally does a longer eye contact, reward with a jackpot and quit.

This lesson is the cornerstone of reform for many dogs. Dogs with control issues typically do not want to—or think that they need to—look to their owners for anything. Changing that mindset takes time, and it's best to progress at your dog's pace.

If He Won't Watch

Some dogs seemingly make progress with the *watch* command, only to suddenly start not wanting to make eye contact.

Oftentimes, the dog has thought things over and decided he doesn't want to give in. If this happens with your dog, you need to persist with the training outlined earlier. If your dog still seems reluctant to comply, you might want to upgrade the treats you are using for ones he likes better, and make sure that he is hungry before the lesson. You can even hold out your dog's food bowl when it's time to feed him, and wait until he makes eye contact before putting the food bowl down. If he refuses, set the food on the counter and walk away. Come back in 15 minutes and ask again. Your dog won't starve if he doesn't get fed for a few hours, and dogs who are determined to maintain their command may hold out for a while. Be prepared to reward for a mere glance, then work up to more.

Leash Control

Puppies tend to follow, but oftentimes adolescent dogs want to bound ahead of their owners and explore the world. This is especially an issue with underexercised dogs, high-drive dogs, and dogs who want to take charge. Teaching your dog to heel alongside of you will help with control issues. Although dogs who are pulling may not be doing so to gain leadership, letting a

Leash control is essential with a hard-to-train dog.

dog lunge ahead on a leash does relinquish your control. So if your dog pulls ahead of you on the leash and will not pay any attention to your commands, teaching him to heel—stay by your side—may help bring him back under control.

Heel

1. Find a place with few distractions.
2. Use a piece of food to hold along your side, and lure your dog into the *heel* position. In formal classes, people want the dog on the handler's left, with the dog's right shoulder adjacent to the handler's left knee. This kind of positioning isn't necessary if you aren't showing your dog in a class. I often practice a dog on both sides because I often walk more than one dog.
3. Begin walking, and reward your dog intermittently with a treat, using another treat to lure him alongside you.
4. When your dog starts walk beside you consistently, begin fading the treat.
5. Once he understands the heel, take him to a more distracting environment.
6. When the distractions start and he pulls ahead, redirect his attention with a treat and bring him back alongside you.

When Distractions Are Stronger Than the Lure of a Treat

Your dog may be determined to plunge ahead of you, in spite of the treat you have to offer. A good technique to use with this problem is to change directions. When you first do this lesson, you may want to go to a park where an erratic path is easier to accommodate and where there are a lot of distractions.

1. Begin walking with your dog by your side.
2. If he pulls ahead and ignores you, turn and walk the other way.
3. Hold the leash firmly, and when the slack is taken up in the leash, keep walking. Let your motion create a natural resistance if your dog tries to forge ahead.
4. If he keeps trying to go ahead of you and you find that the leash is always tight, do an about-face.
5. It may take several practices, but soon your dog will learn to keep an eye on you, and your changes of direction will stop the forward pulling.
6. If you happen to pull your dog to a stop, don't take a step forward until the leash is slack. He must understand that a slack leash is needed when moving forward.

Dealing With the Chronic Leash Puller

Often, when a dog reaches early adolescence, the world becomes extremely distracting and he may pick up the habit of leash pulling, despite your best training efforts. If your dog pulls too much and too often, using a regular collar to try to control him can damage his throat. Although some trainers use corrections with a choke chain to stop the pulling, I feel that turning to a nonpulling device can be a better solution. The following is an overview of some different devices that may work to correct the chronic leash puller.

Traditional Dog Harnesses

A traditional dog harness is a device where the leash attaches in between the dog's shoulder blades. Harnesses won't harm a dog's neck or throat, but these devices don't help prevent or retrain a dog from pulling. With a small dog, a harness can be used to maintain control. However, with larger dogs, it's easier to lose control, be pulled off your feet, or suffer from arm and shoulder strains.

Specialty No-Pull Harnesses

There are several specialty no-pull harnesses. My favorite of them all is the Gentle Leader Easy Walk Harness (or other harnesses with a similar design), which can be used as a retraining device. This looks like a regular harness except that the pull ring is attached to the dog's chest area. The position of the leash allows the dog handler to stop a dog's forward motion when the dog pulls against the leash—the pulling turns the dog, which stops the forward motion and naturally redirects the dog toward his handler. It can be used to break a dog's attention away from a distraction and helps teach him not to pull forward but to instead redirect his attention to his owner. The design of the device also allows the dog's handler more leverage with a strong animal. A no-pull harness, used with positive

Chronic leash pullers should be taught to heel alongside their owners.

reinforcement, can teach a dog to walk alongside his owner without pulling. Be aware that some types of harnesses with thin strapping can quickly rub away hairs from a dog's coat, leaving bare spots or sores.

Head Halters

Head halters look like horse halters—they have a strap that goes around the neck and one that goes over the nose. Head halters are not muzzles and will not prevent a dog from biting. This device, when fitted properly, allows a dog to open his mouth to eat, drink, pant, fetch, bark, and even bite.

There are pros and cons to using head halters. A head halter offers more control than a collar. Many dogs will instinctively pull against a pressure on their neck or shoulders. The head halter not only stops the forward motion, but the pressure at the back of the head when the device is engaged works against the dog's instinct to pull. The snug fit around the neck affects a dog psychologically; the pressure at the back of the neck seems to trigger a natural relaxation instinct and has a calming effect. Some trainers have found that the device is useful in interrupting unwanted behaviors as well, which can give the dog handler a chance to redirect her dog toward a different behavior. In

Head halters may help a dog who pulls on his leash (left).
A specialty no-pull harness (below) allows a dog handler more control with a strong dog.

addition, a few trainers have noticed that when they use a head halter on a dog who is acting aggressive, the dog seems to become a little calmer.

Opponents say that most dogs find the head halter unnatural and uncomfortable, and dogs will fight against the device. Also, if a dog is jerked suddenly by the leash attached to the head halter, and his neck is pulled sharply to the side, he might sustain a neck injury. If you choose to use this training device, you must never suddenly jerk the head halter.

Some trainers don't see this device as any more intrusive to a dog than a regular collar once he learns to accept it. To be honest, some dogs will fight a regular collar, trying to scratch or rub it off until they get used to it. I find halters useful and have seen service dogs trained with them. One service dog handler told me that it was an easy way to guide the dog where not to put his nose.

There are many brands of head halters, such as the Halti and the Gentle Leader Headcollar. If you choose to use these devices, make sure that they are fitted properly—ask a professional for a demonstration on how to use and fit a head halter correctly.

Head Halter Success Story

I once had an older man in one of my puppy classes who had severe arthritis, and his Cairn Terrier's pulling hurt his hands and shoulders. Although the dog heeled fine in class, the man was unable to keep the dog from pulling when walking in the park. The man was quite distressed because he had gotten the dog so that he could have company on his daily walks. At that time, I was just experimenting with using head halters on dogs, and I gave the man a Halti to try; he reported that it worked great. He was able to walk his dog without any pain in his hands because his dog didn't pull when wearing the Halti.

Some dogs will sulk when this device is first used, but I've never seen a dog hurt from sulking—besides, some dogs will sulk simply because they're not in charge. But the consequences of an owner not taking charge can lead to a dog losing walking privileges or even abandonment. To cut down on sulking with a dog wearing a head halter, I immediately distract him by going on a brisk walk or doing something he enjoys.

Chapter Five

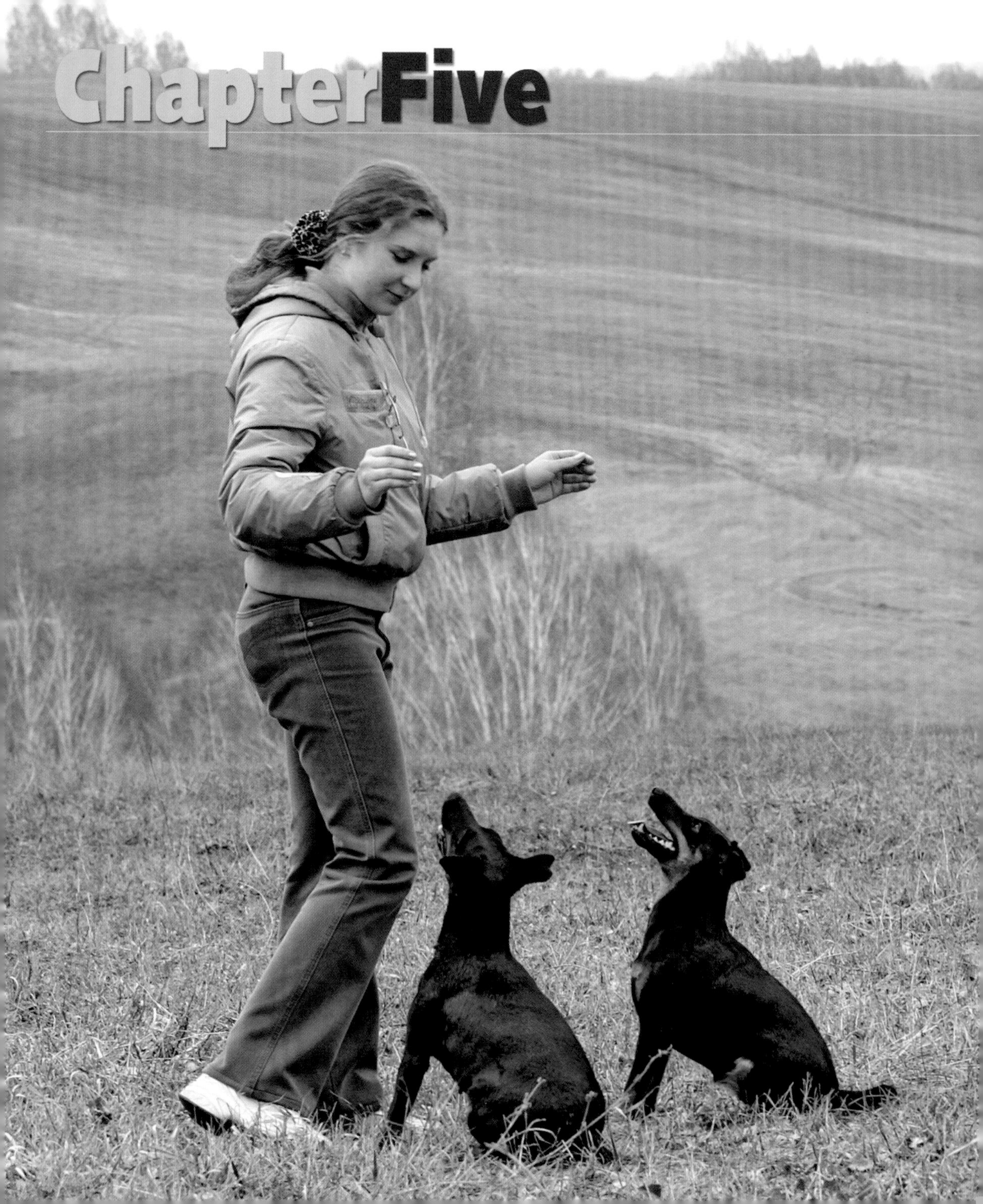

Power Training

Once you've completed the basic training in Chapter 4, you should have a good idea how to work out some of your dog's more resistant or stubborn attitudes. The next step is what I call power training, which goes beyond the basics and uses training to establish yourself as your dog's leader. It replaces the old idea of jerking on a lead and trying to dominate a hard-to-train dog, and it works better, too!

I use this type of training on all dogs because it works to clearly establish the owner as the leader. From stubborn and assertive dogs to shy dogs who need more self-confidence, all can do well with power training. By using these techniques, you'll assure your dog that by following you, his world will be kept in order, which creates security—and most dogs like to know that there's a leader in charge. Even a more assertive dog, who by nature can't seem to help but test his owner, will bond more strongly to a human who takes charge. In short, these exercises are great for all dogs, not just the ones who are trying to control their owners.

Sit-Stay and Down-Stay

By teaching your dog to stay, you are taking charge of his movements. Because he must wait for your permission to move, you become his leader.

There are many ways to teach a dog to stay. Although most people typically train the *sit-stay* first, the *down-stay* is often the easier of the two to train. Both can be taught using similar techniques.

Training the *sit-stay* takes patience and consistency.

Sit-Stay

This exercise will take patience and consistency on your part.

1. Put your dog in a sit on your left side.
2. Place your left hand in front of his face and say "Stay."
3. Step away from your dog with your right foot first and move to the front of your dog.
4. Step back to his side, then release and praise.
5. Once he gets the idea that he needs to stay put, repeat the previous steps, but take a step or two away from your dog.
6. Then work toward taking more steps away from your dog.
7. If he breaks the stay, return him back into position and repeat the command.
8. If he continues to break the stay, be quick to use the leash to return him to the stationary position.

This same technique can also be used for teaching a *down-stay*, only you must put your dog in the down position instead of the *sit*.

Down-Stay

My favorite way to train for a long *down-stay* is one I learned from a woman who worked to train bomb-sniffing dogs.

1. Ask your dog to lie down.
2. When he settles into a *down* position, give him a treat about every ten seconds while saying "Good down."
3. After about a minute, give a release

The Effects of the Down-Stay

When a dog accepts a subordinate position like the *down-stay*, he is relinquishing power to his owner. For this reason, many dog trainers try to force the *down-stay* position by shoving a dog back onto the floor if he tries to break the position before a release word is given. There is no reason to use force for this command. The technique I describe still achieves the benefits of the subordinate position without the dog feeling forced or intimidated—which is especially important when working with a highly sensitive dog. Many strong-willed, high-drive, and stubborn dogs need to be trained to comply, and commands like this can give you a foothold.

---

word like "okay," and walk away.

4. In the next session, if your dog seems to understand how to earn those treats by staying in the *down* position, you can extend the time before rewarding your dog.
5. At this point, you can also begin to take a step or two away from your dog.
6. If he starts to get up when you move away, repeat the *down* command and once again reward for the correct behavior.
7. Soon you should be able to increase both time and distance, with your dog holding the *down-stay* for several minutes.

Power Training

89

You can also use this same basic technique for teaching a *sit-stay*—simply substitute the *down* with the *sit*.

Adding Extra Power to the Sit- and Down-Stay

Once your dog knows the *sit-* and *down-stay*, you can add a little extra power to your training.

1. Attach a leash to your dog.
2. Put your dog in a *sit* position (or *down*) next to you, and stand on the leash.
3. Tell your dog "Stay."
4. Next, toss a treat a short distance away.
5. If your dog breaks the *stay*, the leash will prevent him from getting that treat.
6. Put your dog back into his *sit* and tell him again "Stay."
7. Once your dog settles into his *sit* and accepts that he can't go after the food, give him a release word like "okay" and let him have the treat.

Once your dog gets the idea that he can't

The *down-stay* helps with a dog who doesn't want to give up control to his owner.

have the treat until he receives a release word from you, add more power to this exercise. Schedule some extra time in case you need it.

1. Put your dog into a *sit-* or *down-stay*.
2. Toss a treat and wait for him to look at you before you give the release word.
3. Reward him for just a glance, but then begin to ask for longer looks before you release him.

Ideally, you will not have to wait as long as you did when you first taught the *watch* command. (See Chapter 4.) This exercise can help put you back in charge of your dog. It helps you take control of the food and teaches him to look at you for guidance when he wants something.

Give, Drop It, and Leave It

Among other things, a leader controls food and possessions. Teaching your dog to give up whatever he has in his mouth will help him view you as his leader. Some people run over to their dog, yelling "No!" to get him to drop what he has in his mouth. Instead, teach the *leave it*, *drop it*, and *give* commands so that your dog will understand exactly what you want while you maintain control.

Give

The *give* and *drop it* commands seem similar on the surface because both involve getting your dog to release something in his mouth. However, unlike the *drop it* command (see next section), I use the *give* command to tell a dog to give up a

Using the Stay Command to Control Who Goes First

Don't let your dog barge out the door in front of you. While he may just be enthusiastic about going for a walk, he is taking charge by going first. Also, allowing him to exit in such an excited state of mind makes it hard to get him under control once you are outside of the house. Instead of letting your dog drag you over the threshold, teach him that he must sit by the door and look at you before he is given permission to go outside. Ideally, you'll then precede your dog out the door. If you want to let your dog go first, that's fine, as long as you practice this control technique.

toy to me, but the play will continue with it. This technique helps with a dog who loves playing because it lets him know that his choice to relinquish control of the toy doesn't mean that he will have to stop doing something he loves. This is why when teaching the *give* command, I praise and then reward the dog by quickly throwing the toy again. Most dogs quickly learn not to fight giving up the toy. Then, the last time I take the toy away, I offer a treat as a consolation prize.

To teach the *give* command:

1. Offer a treat in trade for whatever your dog has in his mouth.
2. Praise by saying "Good" when he gives it up.

Drop it

Unlike the *give* command, the *drop it* command typically means that that's the last the dog will see of what he has in his mouth.

1. Give your dog a toy or a chew bone (like a Nylabone).
2. Say "Drop it" while showing him a very tasty treat—make sure that the treat you offer is more desirable than the item you are taking away.
3. Point the treat toward your dog's nose, and hold it until he drops the toy.
4. Praise and give the treat.
5. When your dog drops the toy, immediately give it back to him and repeat the exercise.
6. By giving the toy back, your dog will learn not to worry about relinquishing things in his mouth when asked.
7. After three times, give your dog the toy and walk away without requesting that he drop it.

Drop it indicates that the dog must relinquish what is in his mouth.

Leave It

You can use the *leave it* command when your dog is approaching something he wants to eat or pick up that you don't want him to. For example, because I have horses, I often use the *leave it* command when my dog sees a fresh pile of road apples (horse droppings). If he discovers this pasture treat before me and is already engaged in the delight (at least, it is to him), I use the *drop it* command.

1. Place a toy or chew bone, like a Nylabone, on the floor.
2. Put your dog on a leash.
3. Walk by the desired object.
4. When he starts to go after the chew bone or toy, say "Leave it," and keep walking. The leash should be short enough so your dog has to follow.
5. When your dog redirects his attention to you, give him a treat.
6. With the first lesson, say the command at the same time you use the leash to lead your dog away.
7. The next time you walk by the toy and say the command, hesitate to give your dog a chance to come over to you on his own.
8. If he doesn't, use the leash to lead him away.
9. Continue to give your dog a chance to choose to comply, and don't forget to reward even if you need to pull him away from the treat.
10. Once your dog learns to abandon what he is told to leave, practice the command without a leash.

Using a Drag Leash

With some dogs, leaving a drag leash attached during training can help ensure control. For example, some dogs quickly figure out how to run away from their owners. This not only causes safety issues, but for the owner, it also represents a loss of leadership points. If your dog has this kind of an issue, use a drag leash to take back control.

A drag leash can be a useful tool for training, but don't leave your dog unattended when he's wearing it.

To use a drag leash, put a regular collar on your dog and attach a 6 foot (2 m) leash. If you are outside or in an area where your dog has more room to run, you can use a longer leash or a rope up to 25 feet (8 m) long.

Three Nevers!

Before you start, there are three "never do's" with using a drag leash.

#1: *Never use a drag leash to catch your dog and then punish him.*

Don't use punishment to train your dog, especially when training with a drag leash.

Any harsh treatment associated with using a drag leash can make your dog feel trapped, causing him to become neurotic, or he may even feel forced into defending himself and bite. This device is used to help stop unwanted behaviors, not punish a dog.

#2: *Never leave your dog unattended with a drag leash attached.*

The leash could become tangled on furniture or other household items, so make sure that you keep an eye on him when using a drag leash.

#3: *Never loom over your dog when you catch him.*

Teach your dog to move off the furniture whenever you ask.

A sensitive dog or one who is lower in pack status may submissively urinate if you loom over him, and a young or insecure dog may become too frightened. Instead of looming, grab the end of the leash and use it to stop the unwanted behavior with a gentle pull. If you are using the drag leash to catch your dog, merely step on the rope to keep him from escaping you. Then pick up the end of the leash and call your dog to you. If he doesn't come, even when lured with a treat, use the leash to guide him to you. Give a gentle tug, along with your request to come, and then use the leash to reel him in. Eventually your dog will understand that he can't escape and will let you catch him. Because you never punish your dog after bringing him to you, he will learn that coming—even when he did something wrong—will not mean punishment, and therefore he may be more willing to do so in the future.

Off and Move

A dog who sees himself as in charge will not move off your couch when you tell him. He will also want you to walk around him or step over him. If you are having control issues with your dog, don't move around him—make him move. Use a drag leash to enforce your command, but remember, don't leave your dog unattended with that drag leash. Instead, plan for a time when you notice that your dog tends to lie in a certain spot, such as after he eats.

On Whose Terms?

When dealing with an assertive dog, expect him to try to get things he wants on his terms. Because of his nature, an assertive dog will want to take control. He needs to learn that the fastest way to get what *he* wants is to do what *you* want. Don't punish your dog for trying things his way; just use training (and patience) to get him to realize that you are not going to compromise.

1. Attach a drag leash to your dog.
2. Take hold of the drag leash, show him a treat, then ask him to move by using the *off* or *move* command.
3. If he moves, reward him with the treat.
4. If he does not respond to your command, use the leash to physically move him. You can still reward him with the treat when he moves to where you want him.
5. Then drop the leash and walk away.
6. Do this a couple times before you end the lesson.
7. The next day, when you do this lesson, give your dog a few seconds to let him decide to move on his own.
8. Some dogs may wiggle a little, then decide not to move after all.
9. If your dog wiggles, then seems to be settling back down, simply pull him off the area with the leash.

Please note: *If you have a dog who threatens you by growling or snapping when you ask him to move, get professional help*. Although some experienced people may feel comfortable working with a more threatening dog and can bring a dog who snaps at them back under control, don't hesitate to seek help if you feel any apprehension or have concerns.

This kind of retraining goes better if you have done your basic obedience work, which helps chip away at a dog's power. As mentioned earlier, dogs tend to gain power a little at a time. You can take away their power and assert your leadership by using the same concept.

You Control the Treats

Because of their persistent nature, assertive dogs seem to slip into controlling roles quite easily. Even with basic training and the addition of power training, you may still find your dog trying to take charge. Occasionally, this happens when training with treats, where your dog may solicit you for a treat or run "treat blackmail." Both problems allow him to take control in a situation in which you should be maintaining control.

Soliciting a Treat

It isn't unusual for more assertive or dominant dog to ask for a treat or a reward by putting his paws on you, lunging at the treat, jumping up on you, attempting to snatch the treat from your hand, barking, or whining. Instead of focusing on the command you asked for, these dogs will concentrate on getting that treat—on their terms. You certainly don't need to punish your dog for these kinds of behaviors, but you do need to make sure that you never reward him when he demands a treat. You must also take charge with this issue through training. The best way to train with a demanding dog is to refuse to acknowledge any actions he takes to get the treat on his terms.

1. Start by pulling out a treat.
2. Ask your dog to sit.

Daisy (see story in box, right) loved to solicit for a treat.

Daisy Wanted to Be in Charge

Daisy, a Miniature Schnauzer who could learn commands quickly, just as quickly decided that she wasn't going to do what she was told. Daisy's not a dominant dog, but because of her assertive nature, she often looked for opportunities to take charge.

She liked to solicit a treat by jumping up on her owner, Michelle. To counter this problem, Michelle trained Daisy to sit to get a treat. At first, Daisy cooperated, but then she started to take charge by holding the *sit* for an instant and then demanding the treat by jumping and grabbing at it.

To help bring Daisy back under control, we added more power to the lesson by asking for the *watch* command after the *sit*.

Step 1: Lengthen the time Daisy sat. Michelle asked for a *sit* and gave Daisy treats in 15-second intervals while saying "Good sit." Then Michelle gave a release word and walked away. Michelle began to lengthen the time in between the reward for the *sit*, until Daisy could hold still for almost a minute.

Step 2: Get Daisy to learn to watch Michelle to get the treat. Michelle would hold out the treat but would not give it for a mere *sit*—she waited until Daisy made eye contact. The eye contact was rewarded immediately with a "Yes," followed by the treat. Daisy learned that she had to glance at her owner for the treat, but at first she would only make a quick glance. To gain more control, Michelle asked for more and more eye contact. When Daisy merely gave a quick glance, only verbal encouragement (a "Yes") was given but no treat. After a second glance, Michelle rewarded her dog.

Step 3: Work on Daisy's regression. This technique can work well on many dogs— except Daisy had other ideas. After a few lessons, instead of glancing at Michelle, Daisy went back to jumping to get the treat.

There are a few ways to handle this kind of regression. The first is to end the lesson without giving any treat. Typically, after a few times, a dog will often decide that you are not going to compromise on the rules for getting the treat and will try things your way. If, after two times of quitting the lesson, your dog is still not watching you, go back to Step 1, where you rewarded every 15 seconds for maintaining a *sit*. On the next lesson, repeat Step 1 and then move on to Step 2 (asking for the *watch* command). Depending on how invested your dog is on controlling this issue, you may need to insist that he make eye contact for several lessons before he gives in.

While Daisy did regress a time or two, with persistence from Michelle, she finally gave up and decided that the quickest way to get that treat was to sit and stare at her owner.

Power Training

3. Ignore any of his unwanted behaviors, like barking, whining, and pawing.

4. Don't react to any action your dog takes except for the *sit* that you asked for.

5. Every so often, repeat the command to sit, but don't repeat the word more than once every half minute.

6. Be firm about not rewarding your dog for any action except the one you asked for.

Expect this first lesson to take some time. Depending on how tenacious your dog is and if he's gotten away with misbehaviors before, this can take less than a minute. However, with some dogs, I've had to wait several minutes.

If your dog doesn't know the command for *sit*, you can still use this method by withholding the reward until he does something you want him to do.

1. Pull out a treat.

2. Ignore unwanted behaviors, and wait until your dog offers a behavior you do want.
   - With a smaller dog who is jumping, you could acknowledge the moment he has all four feet on the ground by saying "Yes" and giving him the treat.
   - With a larger dog, he may happen to sit in an attempt to paw at you—acknowledge the *sit* with the word "yes" and reward, but try to reward the *sit* before he paws you. (Otherwise, you'll inadvertently reward the bad behavior.)

3. Don't be surprised if your dog does a little experimenting to try to get that treat by persisting in pawing or offering other behaviors.

4. Wait patiently until you get the behavior you want.

5. Eventually, your dog will repeat the desired action if you acknowledge and reward it consistently.

Allow yourself some time when teaching your dog not to solicit a treat. Sometimes you may have to wait almost five minutes before he offers a behavior you can reward.

If your dog is running treat blackmail, try asking for more than one thing, like a sit, then down.

Don't stop after the first success—allow your dog to earn at least three rewards, then stop the lesson. In the second lesson, try to achieve a total of five rewards. In the third training session, if your dog is quick to cooperate, let him earn two rewards and then move on to some new training.

Even a dog who takes some time for the first success will eventually come to the conclusion that the quickest way to get what he wants—the treat—is to do what you want.

Running Treat Blackmail

"Watch this, the dog has me trained." Larry picked up a treat and asked Kelsey to jump up in his lap. Kelsey complied. "Now watch this." Larry put Kelsey down and again asked her to jump on his lap but this time without holding a treat. Kelsey looked at Larry and cocked her head as if she didn't understand. He then said, "I can't even fake her out." He pretended to pick up a treat and asked her to jump up. Kelsey again cocked her head as if she didn't understand. "Now watch." Larry took a treat from the table and told Kelsey "Up." She immediately jumped into his lap.

If your dog has the attitude "no treat, no trick," then you are the victim of treat blackmail. A dog running treat blackmail has taken charge, and it's up to you to regain control. Here are a few techniques to regain control of a blackmailing dog.

Ask for More Than One Thing

Dogs running treat blackmail will not perform a command unless they see the treat. If your dog has this habit, try the following:

1. Hold out the treat and ask for a command, but before you hand over that treat, ask for another task. For example, ask for a *sit*, then after he sits, ask for a *down*.
2. If your dog won't perform the *down*, use the treat to lure him into the *down* position.
3. Reward after the second task, but begin adding more and more requests each time you practice, such as asking for a series of *sits* and *downs* before giving the treat.

The key is to use only *one* treat as a reward for a series of tasks.

Train With Treats Out of Sight

To break your dog of his blackmailing habit, you can also train him without the

Try training with the treats out of sight to stop your dog from soliciting them.

treat in sight. There are several steps to training your dog to work without seeing the treat. For session one:

1. Show him a treat, then set it down on your kitchen counter.
2. Ask for a *sit*.
3. If he doesn't sit without you holding the treat, pick up the treat and again ask for a *sit*.
4. Once he sits, set the treat on the counter for a moment, pick it back up, praise with a "Good sit," and then toss him the treat.

This can be a long process for some dogs. Practice once or twice for the first session, then give your dog some time to think it over. Start session two the next day:

1. Show your dog the treat, set it down on the counter, and then ask for a *sit*.
2. Be persistent—you may have to work for several short sessions before your dog is willing to do your bidding without you holding the treat.
3. If your dog is completely uncooperative, leave the treat on the counter and walk away.

If your dog is running treat blackmail, try hiding treats throught the house and then practicing commands.

4. After a short time, start the process over again.
5. Once he decides to cooperate, start asking for more than one task before awarding the treat.

Hide Treats Throughout the House

Another way to train with treats out of sight is to set them throughout the house. It's a similar process to training with the treat on the counter.

Taking Back Control Happens a Little at a Time

Training sessions that help you regain control, like the ones taught in this chapter, are best kept relatively short. With each session you can ask for a little more from your dog, but it's best to stop the training session once you get one or two correct actions. Look for some improvement, but don't expect that all dogs will move along this path quickly. With these kinds of lessons, you are not teaching your dog a new trick—you are asking a strong-willed dog to learn to comply.

1. Choose a room, and with your dog out of the way, place treats around. (I put mine on kitchen counters and dressers in my bedroom.)
2. Have your dog follow you to the "treat" room.
3. Stand close to a place where you've hidden a treat, and ask for a *sit*.
4. If he doesn't comply, pick up the treat, show it to him, return it to where it was hidden, and again ask for a *sit*.
5. Keep working with this lesson until your dog gets into the habit of sitting on command before he sees the treat.
6. Once you achieve compliance, fade the treats.

Power Training

Chapter Six

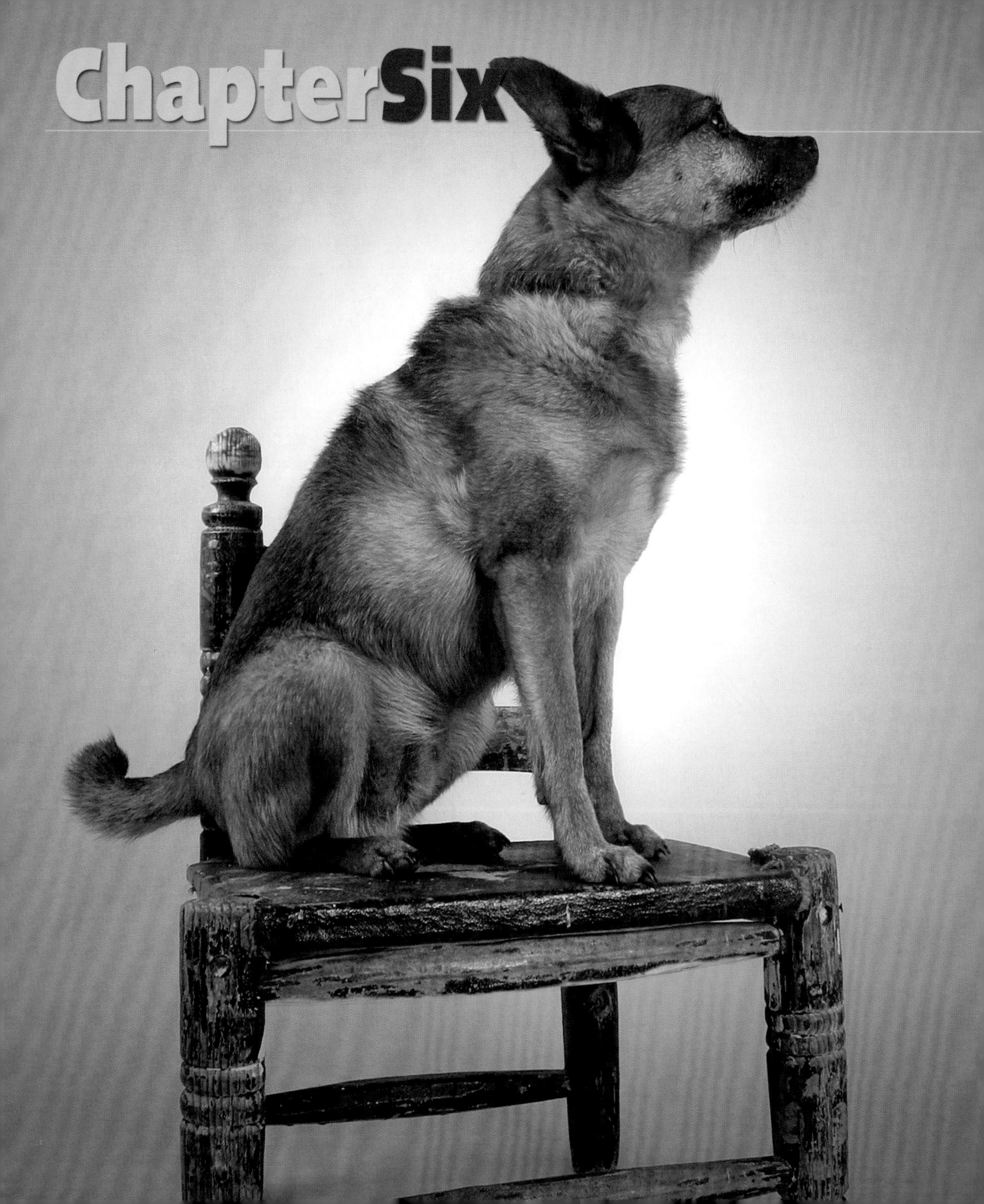

Upping the Stakes

There are dogs who are trained to sit, stay, leave it, drop it, and come when called, only to fail to come when chasing after a car or refuse to drop a particularly tasty piece of garbage. In the past, the traditional way to deal with this kind of misbehavior was to resort to physical punishment to gain compliance. After all, the dog knew the *come* command but obviously defied his owner and therefore "deserved" to be punished. But physical punishment is not a good idea—it creates more problems than it solves.

Using physical punishment to correct misbehaviors causes many counterproductive reactions in dogs. All too often, the punishment is awarded after the crime, which leaves it to the dog to figure out why he was punished. Overly sensitive dogs will focus on the punishment and forget about the crime. Punishment also breaks down the bond between owner and dog, and some dogs will employ avoidance behavior when physically punished, which means that they will find a way to continue the misbehavior and avoid the unwanted consequences.

Although the first step is always training a dog to do what you want, I believe that there are times when a dog needs to be corrected, because if he is allowed to misbehave, the owner will lose control of that dog. Often, the key to compliance is about finding the right technique for your dog. The right technique depends on the relationship you have with your pet and his basic personality. For many owners, finding a way to get their dog to comply is hard work. However, by using a step-by-step process and building on solid obedience training (found in Chapter 4), a dog can be taught to comply.

Finding the Right Way to Correct Unwanted Behaviors

"Upping the Stakes" is my version of a technique called "Climbing the Ladder," which was introduced to me by a trainer named Jay Blanchard. Jay's idea of Climbing the Ladder was to use progressively discouraging techniques by increasing the negativity of the

Using physical punishment to correct misbehaviors creates many counterproductive reactions in dogs.

consequences for the misbehavior. I've modified that concept in my Upping the Stakes technique. I start by using positive reinforcement, move on to using insistence, and then add discouragement. The discouragement I use is something that a dog will regret but that doesn't engage in a physically harsh action.

The Upping the Stakes approach can help you find the best solution for correcting a dog. Although Upping the Stakes begins with positive training, sometimes more than positive training is needed because some misbehaviors are more rewarding than any treat an owner can offer. For this reason, I offer different approaches for owners to try when resolving compliance issues. By progressing through a hierarchy, an owner can often find the best solution while at the same time keeping the training as positive as possible.

Force Versus Enforce

In the following discussion, when I talk about "forcing" a dog to do something, I mean physically making him comply. For example, if your dog won't sit with the lure of a treat, you may help guide him into a *sit* position. This kind of forcing may be done to enforce your command, but it shouldn't be harsh. Once your dog is sitting, you can still reward him, even though he needed a lot of assistance. A great way to change unwanted behaviors is to find a way to get your dog to do a behavior you can reward rather than to punish him for doing something you don't want. The best way to train your dog is to be a smart leader and use no more force than necessary.

When I refer to "enforcing," I mean what a good leader would do to make sure that rules are followed. Again, this doesn't mean using harsh techniques. Enforcing a command can be as simple as using your leash to prevent your dog from going forward and breaking the *stay* command.

Technique Overlap

When using Upping the Stakes, taking a little of each of the three training steps can often help with compliance. The sections on "Technique Overlap" deal with examples where a bit of the previous technique is combined with the next technique as a good way to gain compliance.

Step 1: Compliance Through Reward

The first step of Upping the Stakes uses rewards to get a dog to choose to comply. Compliance through reward is what we used in the basic training chapter and should always be the first technique you try when training.

There is always an element of choice in compliance—even if that choice is out of fear of the consequences of punishment. If you force a dog to sit by shoving his behind downward when you ask him to perform the command, that dog has chosen to comply under your force. I came to realize this when watching someone working with a Shiba Inu. When he tried to force the dog's behind down, the dog jerked back on the leash and thrashed. He never did get that dog to sit because the dog had chosen to fight rather than to comply.

Stubborn and independent dogs will have the tendency to fight compliance when force is used as a training technique. With these dogs, training by facilitating the dog's choice

105

to comply works better than trying to force the dog to choose compliance.

Compliance Through Reward With Drop It

Training the *drop it* command, which was discussed in Chapter 5, is a good example of how Compliance Through Reward is used. Instead of punishing your dog for having something in his mouth that you wanted him to drop, you rewarded him for doing what you wanted when he dropped the item. You learned how to train for what you want rather than punish for what you don't want. After your dog complied with your command, you rewarded him with a treat, some praise, or both.

Using the First Step Correctly

Many people find that by using Compliance Through Reward correctly, they can solve a lot of their dogs' behavior issues. The following scenario is designed to help illustrate how to better use this technique.

If your dog is exhibiting problem behaviors around bike riders, the proper use of the Compliance Through Reward method can help stop these behaviors.

Training the Hard-to-Train Dog

Snappy and the Bike

Let's say that your dog Snappy has a problem behavior. When he sees a bike, he whines, gets anxious, and if given the chance, will chase that bike and grab at the rider's ankles. You, being a smart owner, do some power training with him, which works to teach him to trust your decisions in matters where he previously took charge. With power training out of the way, you are ready to change Snappy's unwanted behavior by using Step 1: Compliance Through Reward.

You begin your reform by arranging for a bike rider to assist you. With your pockets filled with treats and Snappy on a leash, you are ready to redirect the unwanted behavior. When the bike rider approaches, Snappy begins to whine and show anxiety. When the bike gets closer, you tell Snappy to sit while offering him a treat. Unfortunately, he doesn't sit but runs to the end of the leash and tries to get the bike, the very behavior you wanted to reform. But before you decide to up the stakes and move on to Step 2 to solve this issue, let's reexamine your technique and where you may have failed.

The first mistake was that you asked Snappy for a *sit* too late. When he whined and began to behave anxiously, he was already deciding how to react to that bike. Snappy was just waiting for the bike to get close enough to launch an all-out attack. A better time to ask your dog to sit is when he first notices the bike but before he begins to act upset by it. What you want to teach him is that when he sees a bike, he should sit and look at you. That behavior will replace his current one of getting upset and chasing and biting.

Another possible mistake at this stage is that some people don't adequately teach their dogs how to sit on command in a distracted area. Dogs are often willing to sit and focus on their owners when in the house, but when outside around many distractions, they may need additional work to focus. Practice getting your dog to focus on you in the training area before you introduce the bike. Also, to help redirect your dog's attention to you and away from the bike, don't hesitate to feed one treat after another in the beginning stages to help maintain his attention on you. As you find success, you can slow down your delivery of treats.

If you have a dog who readily sits and focuses on you when he first sees the bike but still gets upset as the bike gets closer, modify your technique. Find a distance at which he will not behave adversely to the bike in motion. Have him sit and focus on you at that distance for a few passes with the bike. Now take him a few steps closer, and have him sit and focus on you. If your dog accepts this closer distance, again take him a little closer. Stop the lesson at this point. The next day, start from a distance you already know he's comfortable with, and ask for a *sit*. If he does well, you can again proceed closer to the bike. Only ask for a little less distance from the bike each lesson. This kind of desensitization takes several lessons to achieve but can work for many dogs.

You can also try having the bike stop the moment the dog gets upset, and then the two of you can slowly approach the stationary bike. While approaching, stop a few times and ask your dog to sit and focus on you. When you finally reach the bike and rider, have the rider feed your dog a treat. Once he relaxes around the bike, praise him and take him away from it. Don't have the bike rider leave you or the motion may upset your dog. Eventually, after your dog feels at ease approaching the bike once it stops, allow it to roll a few steps away and monitor your dog's reaction. Although this process takes time, by working at your dog's comfort level, you will eventually get him to learn to tolerate the bike and rider at any distance.

This kind of retraining will go faster with some dogs than others. Dogs who have a lot of fears and anxieties, or dogs who have had the behavior issue for a while, may take more effort to retrain and reform. If you have a dog who has a lot of fear-based issues, don't work on all of them at once. Instead, choose one to conquer first. It may take a lot of time, but after that first one is

Your goal when training is to have your dog choose to comply with your command.

conquered, your dog will learn to trust you in these matters and will often get over other fear issues more quickly.

By the way, his actions of whining and behaving anxiously indicate that although something like prey drive may have initiated his original response to chase the bike, somewhere along the line, he has probably become a little frightened of that bike and rider. Often, dogs who show some fear in their unwanted behavior work better with a redirection technique than some of the other compliance steps listed in the following sections. The steps listed later more often work with a defiant dog who has decided that he doesn't want to comply.

Step 2: Compliance Through Insistence

Compliance Through Insistence is the one technique that I've had the greatest success with when correcting unwanted behaviors. This technique doesn't rely on using harsh training methods to force a dog to comply. Instead, you enforce your command by following through to ensure that the dog does as he is told. One of the reasons why this kind of technique works is because dogs accept that the leader of the pack has the right to enforce compliance. In fact, dogs expect a good leader to enforce compliance to be worthy respect. With some dogs, after you insist that they comply a few times, they will begin to choose to comply.

When you make a dog comply, whether by soliciting cooperation or by physically

Use Rewards First

As mentioned earlier, the old style of training taught a dog to sit by using force. Often a choke chain was used to create discomfort until the dog complied. Instead, use the reward method to teach a *sit* rather than punishment until he figures out what he is expected to do.

making him do so, he sees you as a leader. This has a self-perpetuating effect: The dog understands that he must comply because you are the leader, and he sees you as the leader because he must comply. That's the kind of self-perpetuating situation you want.

Not making your dog comply also has a self-perpetuating effect. When he fails to comply, he becomes empowered. He also comes to accept this power as a privilege he can keep. If there is an area where you fail to take command through training, then you are not a successful leader. By training your dog and enforcing commands, you remove the question of who is in charge. When you fail to enforce a command, you tempt your dog to look for other areas in which he can successfully disobey.

With this step, you will:

1. Repeat the command you asked for.
2. Then find a way to make your dog obey.

Don't use this step for initially training your dog to perform a task. If he hasn't been taught to do the task, such as sit on command, you can better achieve compliance using Step 1: Compliance Through Reward.

Compliance Through Insistence for Come Defiance

Let's say that you just called your dog to come, but he is too busy sniffing some great smell on a bush to comply. You've already trained him to come using the reward method. You should walk over, take hold of his collar, repeat your request to come, and lure him to where you previously stood. If he won't be lured with a reward, you'll need to insist on his compliance. With some dogs, a clap of the hand and a sharp mention of their name will cause them to choose to comply. With another type of dog, you'll have to put on his leash, go to the end of the leash, repeat the command, gently pull him to you, and then reward him when he arrives.

Training Isn't Over Until He Chooses to Comply

But the training isn't over for the dog who needed the leash to force compliance. The idea is to have him *choose* to come without you needing to go over and get him. To continue with *come* training, attach a long drag leash. Wait until your dog is distracted, then call for him to come. If he doesn't comply, grab the end of the drag leash and give a gentle tug. If he doesn't come immediately, use a second tug to get him to face you, and then again request that he come while using his name. Repeat with the tugs until he decides to come. If he doesn't come after a few tugs, reel him in again. The next time, repeat the

Repeating a Command

Many dog-training books will tell you to only say a command once. Ideally, when first training a command, only saying that command once is correct. However, when working to get compliance from a dog, sometimes repeating your command works to convince him that you are going to enforce it. This is especially effective if you use a sterner tone and a more assertive body posture the second time you repeat the command. Of course, to really convince your dog that repeating your command means that it will be enforced, you must actually enforce the command the third time you repeat it. Too often, owners continually repeat the command but never enforce it. Three times is the most you should repeat a request.

previous steps and always give your dog the opportunity to comply before you make him.

Don't forget to offer a reward when your dog arrives, even if you had to force his compliance. A reward can help perpetuate his choice to comply, which is very valuable when you are dealing with a dog who has less internal motivation to do so. However, don't expect that your dog will turn around after one or two lessons. Compliance typically takes longer to secure than teaching the initial command because you are trying to create a habit of compliance. And the more rewarding the habit is, the stronger the incentive is to continue it. With cigarette smokers, more than one factor keeps them hooked. It's a habit that often continues without thought, and the cigarette smoker has both psychological and physical

Tracy is using the compliance through insistence method by enforcing the *sit-stay* with her dog Sierra.

incentives to continue. You can give your dog the same kind of incentives (although much healthier ones!) Give him something physical, such as praise and rewards, to get him to form the right habit. To hook him psychologically, you should develop a strong bond. (You'll find some ideas to help you bond with your dog in Chapter 7.)

Sierra Blew Off the Come Command

Tracy Marx started out with all the right training for her Husky, Sierra. She took Sierra everywhere to socialize her and obtained private training lessons to ensure that her dog learned to behave. After all, Tracy had done her research with the breed and knew that Huskies were strong willed, independent, and very smart.

Sierra's training seemed to be successful. She would sit on command, stay, and lie down. Tracy could even call her to come unless she was highly distracted. With Sierra's good manners and solid training, it was no surprise when she earned her Canine Good Citizen award. However, there were hints of growing problems with Sierra. During one agility trial, she ran off the course after taking three jumps and refused to come back when Tracy called.

Tracy had made previous attempts to resolve Sierra's *recall* problem. When Sierra was off leash, Tracy used toys to try to lure her dog back, which didn't work if Sierra lost interest in the toy, and Tracy often ended up catching Sierra by having to trap her. By catching her dog, Tracy did enforce

Firm Tone of Voice and Solid Body Posture

Tone of voice varies from person to person. Someone with soprano tendencies will never sound like a baritone. However, we all go up an octave or two when we are uncertain or afraid. And we can go downward in tone when we are being stern.

Lowering your tone of voice commands more power with some dogs. If your dog is sensitive, try working to make your voice tone sound solid and self-assured. Sometimes it helps to think about how your tone is used to encourage your dog, which can help you find the right solid voice to use. You may want to ask someone to help critique your tone of voice by watching for the dog's reactions.

Solid body posture is more straightforward. For a solid stance, place your feet about shoulder width apart, level your chin, and pull your shoulders back. This kind of powerful position will reassure your dog as well as help enforce your authority.

the command, but she still wasn't having success with getting her dog to reliably come when called.

To resolve the issue, Tracy needed to gain more of Sierra's respect by becoming a stronger leader. Although there are a lot of little things that feed into any dog's compliance issues, Sierra's two biggest issues were bolting out the door and not paying attention to Tracy when distracted.

Although Tracy attempted to prevent Sierra from bolting out the door, unfortunately, the wind blew the door open one day and Sierra ran across the street to a construction site. Tracy pursued and then called the dog to come, but Sierra refused. Finally, Tracy asked a construction worker to call the dog. Sierra readily went to the construction worker, who grabbed her collar.

Sierra was willing to come to a stranger but not to Tracy because she had learned to use avoidance behavior when Tracy called. The dog discovered that by not complying with Tracy's command, she could continue running around and having a good time. For Sierra, noncompliance was more rewarding than compliance. To change that behavior, Tracy needed to convince Sierra that compliance was not an option but a rule. She needed to gain Sierra's respect through stronger leadership training.

Tracy began to turn around Sierra's compliance issue by first working to resolve her habit of bolting out the door. When Sierra took liberties and ran out the door, she was claiming certain leadership rights. By training Sierra so that she couldn't bolt out the door, Tracy put herself in a stronger leadership role.

Tracy set up a specific training routine to resolve the problem. She would go to the door, put Sierra in a *sit* position, and tell her to wait. Then she'd open the door and use a leash to enforce her command if Sierra tried to go out without permission. The dog learned to wait for an "okay" before leaving the house and had to learn to follow Tracy out the door. Tracy even practiced control when it was time to go out to eliminate. Sierra became accustomed to waiting for a command to exit the house, which relinquished leadership back to Tracy and gave her more control of her dog.

Tracy also took more control when she walked Sierra. Like many people, Tracy didn't mind Sierra walking ahead of her when out on a leisurely walk. However, she was aware that making the dog heel alongside her had leadership value. So

Tracy came up with a compromise—she would allow Sierra to walk out in front until something came along that might tempt her dog's attention. When Sierra pulled on the leash, Tracy would make her take the *heel* position and keep her attention on Tracy until the tempting distraction was gone.

When a compliance issue has deeper roots, you must work on more than the issue at hand. Before Sierra could learn to comply with the *come* command, she first needed to learn to comply in other areas that had leadership value. Once Sierra was trained not to barge out of the house and

Using a firm tone and solid body posture will help with compliance training.

once she learned to give Tracy attention when distracted, Tracy was able to have success in training her to come on command

Compliance Through Insistence for Drop It Defiance

Let's use the *drop it* command as an example once again. You've previously taught your dog the *drop it* command using the positive method found in Chapter 5. However, even though your dog knows what "Drop it" means, he sees greater reward in quickly chewing and swallowing what he has in his mouth. Now you have a problem because your dog understands the command but chooses not to obey because of the more immediate reward.

Try Using Two Commands

Let's say that you've given your dog the *leave it* command, but you're not in time or he's already honed in on the forbidden item, and before you know it he has the item in his mouth. Try switching to the *drop it* command. The doubling of your commands—commands that the dog already associates with compliance—will often help your dog choose to finally comply.

Also, calling out two commands will sometimes convince a dog to comply more readily than repeating the one command twice. Use a firm tone of voice and a solid body posture, which will help communicate to your dog that he must comply.

Why Reward a Dog When You Have to Make Him Comply?

There is a benefit in rewarding your dog when you make him comply. More independent dogs must learn to seek rewards through their owners. An independent dog, by nature, tends to be quite resourceful at finding his own means of getting what he wants. Anything you can do to change that mindset is a benefit. By rewarding your dog—even when you force him to comply—you begin to train him to look to you for rewards, an action which makes him a little less independent.

Also, using punishment instead of rewards causes some of the more independent or assertive dogs to revert to avoidance behavior, and highly sensitive dogs may overreact to punishment.

Upping the Stakes if Your Dog Decides not to Comply

Perhaps your dog has decided not to drop what he has in his mouth, even though you used the two command overlap. For simplicity, let's call your dog Sparky. Sparky has decided that there is greater reward in eating the road apple he just picked up. So when you tell him "Drop it," he quickly gobbles down the treat, thus opting for the more immediate reward. Of course, some people might try to punish him after the fact. However, it's a better idea to come up with a way to get compliance without punishment. And besides, your dog may decide that tolerating a harsh reprimand was worth the price of eating that road apple.

Drilling

One way to up the stakes when you have a dog who fails to obey a command he knows is to drill him on that command. It's a good way to not only enforce the command but to give the dog some doubt about choosing not to comply the next time. How many times you may need to drill your dog can vary among individuals, so do a little experimenting. Some dogs will work better if you drill them several times in one lesson, and other dogs work better if you drill them a few times over several lessons.

Setting Up a Training Scenario to Insist on Compliance

Another method to achieve compliance is to set up a situation in which your dog will be tempted to pick up something he shouldn't, but you'll be in a position to intervene. For example, you might put something your dog wants to eat on the floor in your living room. Choose something that he can't eat faster than you can stop him from eating, like a stuffable Nylabone filled with peanut butter. Stuffable Nylabones are designed so he can't consume the peanut butter too quickly.

Once you have your bait ready, put a drag leash on your dog so that you can stop him from escaping your request. Let him approach the treat on his own. (Sometimes

Time-outs can help control unwanted dog behavior and compliance issues.

you may need to turn your back to your dog to get him to take action.) When he picks up the bone and begins to eat the peanut butter, say "Drop it." If your dog doesn't comply immediately, give a tug on the leash and repeat the command. If he still refuses to comply, go over to him and take the bone away. Repeat your command while enforcing his compliance. When you get possession of the bone, praise him and offer a different reward.

Some more tenacious dogs will decide that dropping something inside the house is one thing but out on the street is another.

With this kind of dog, you may need to train in the problem area. Be sure to have a leash attached so that you can enforce your command.

Step 3: Compliance Through Time-Outs, Bartering, and "Missing Out"

For many problems, the Compliance Through Insistence step will turn the tide because it reinforces your leadership. However, we've bred some of our working dogs to have traits that don't fit well with a typical pack structure. Also, some

The Right Amount of Time for Your Dog's Time-Out

The amount of time a dog spends in a time outs will vary with the amount of focus a dog has in general, and how invested he is in doing a particular unwanted behavior. You will find that dogs who have gotten away with things for a long time will often need a longer time out at the beginning of their training. Here are some general guidelines:

- Try fifteen minutes at first. Then do a focus test by asking the dog to do the *watch* command from inside the crate. If the dog makes eye contact, then let him out as a reward. Now take him back into the training situation and see if he will comply.
- If he won't comply, try a thirty minute time out. Again test with the *watch* command before letting him outside that crate.

At this point, many trainers move up to an hour time out. Some will try a two hour time out, but I feel that if an hour doesn't work, I often need to try the task the next day. If there is no success the next day, try a half hour time out the first time, and skip the fifteen minute time out. As the dog improves his behavior, you can begin to reduce the time outs back down to fifteen minutes.

Who Owns the Dog Toys?

When you buy a toy for your dog and give it to him to play with, do you consider it his toy? After all, you specifically chose that toy for your precious dog to enjoy. But the toys in the house do not belong to your dog. He doesn't own anything in the house if you are the leader. You control where he sleeps, all the food, and all the toys. If your dog acts like he "owns" anything, you have given up part of your leadership. So keep those toys put away, and bring them out only when you decide that it's time to play. Remember, your dog needs to understand that you control the toys and you control the playtime; if you don't, you relinquish leadership points that can lead to problem behaviors.

overly assertive and extremely stubborn dogs have behaviors that don't encourage pack harmony. Even some of the more dominant breeds have characteristics that can challenge the normal hierarchy of the pack. Because of this, merely asserting one's authority may not always work.

When working to correct these kinds of dogs using regular training techniques, compliance can become intermittent or nonexistent. Because many of them are bred to outthink other animals and to use avoidance behavior, different training techniques are needed. Time-outs,

bartering, and having the dog "miss out" on something he likes can increase the likelihood of compliance.

The Time-Out Technique

Time-outs can help control unwanted dog behaviors and resolve compliance issues. Time-outs can work because the dog is forced to stop the misbehavior, which lets his owner take back control. Typically, a time-out is done in a crate, which helps keep the dog from going back to the unwanted behavior. The crate also allows him time to stop focusing on his misbehavior. Some of the herding and hunting breeds seem to have a longer focus time, whether it's a required job or an unwanted behavior. Merely stopping this type of dog from engaging in a behavior doesn't disrupt his intention of returning to that behavior as quickly as possible. Taking a time-out helps diffuse his heightened energy and gives him a chance to change his focus.

Often, one of two things happens when a dog emerges from a crate after a time-out. Some will decide that next time, they need to stop when told because they don't like the time-out consequences. Other dogs may decide to try to prevent their owner from stopping them the next time so that they can continue with the unwanted behavior and not lose control. The latter decision is called avoidance behavior.

How long a dog needs to be crated to achieve a change of mind and to stop focusing on the unwanted behavior can vary. Some dogs will not lose focus for a

117

long time. But once a dog has lost focus on the behavior you didn't want, you will have a better chance of getting him to focus on what you do want.

The Bartering Technique

Some dogs are born with a very assertive nature, and this can become a natural obstacle to training. When dealing with some of these more demanding or assertive dogs, try this bartering technique, which includes the "no free lunch" concept. The basis of this technique is that the dog must earn his rewards by complying to a request from his owner first. For example, before you feed your dog, ask for a *sit* before you put down the food bowl.

Another way to use bartering is with play, which some dogs find even more rewarding than food. In fact, some dogs will even try to dominate and take control of playtime by initiating the play or keeping control of the toy. If you find your dog demanding play or your attention, ask him to do something to earn that privilege. This kind of bartering will help keep you in control. If your dog comes over and nudges you to be petted, ask him for a *down* before you give him your attention. If he wants to play and paws at you or brings over a toy, put the toy in front of him and have him wait for you to give a release word to go fetch the toy before you play with it.

It helps to keep all toys put away until you decide to use them with your dog. Most

You can enlist the help of another dog to help your dog learn to relinquish a ball.

dogs do better if they don't have free access to toys, which keeps you in control.

The "Missing Out" Technique

You can also try to get compliance by having your dog "miss out" on something he wants (or wants to do) if he doesn't comply. Let's continue to use play as an example. If you have a dog who won't bring the ball back when playing, try playing with another ball or dog.

First, take out another ball or a toy your dog likes to play with. Call him to get his attention, then throw the other ball. This will help him understand that to continue to play catch, you need a ball to throw. Some dogs will learn to bring the one they have back.

If you own more than one dog (or have access to a friend's dog) who knows how to play fetch, you can also try having the second dog help retrain the problem dog. After throwing your ball, if the problem dog takes off with it and won't bring it back when you ask, take out a second ball and throw that ball to the second dog, who will bring it back. Completely exclude the problem dog from the game until you are done playing, then stop playing for the day.

When I have used this technique, I typically see the problem dog bring the ball back but still persist in trying to dominate the game. If the problem dog brings back the ball, I will throw it for him. If he refuses to bring back the ball a second time, I will not give him another chance until the next play session. Sometimes I will end the play session a little early so that I can offer a play session an hour later to give the problem dog another chance. I typically see problem dogs take five or six lessons to reform when using this technique.

Technique Overlap

Let's continue to use the example of reforming a dog who wants to control playtime. You've tried Step 1: Compliance Through Reward, but your dog finds controlling the play much more rewarding than anything you can offer. Next, it's time to try Step 2: Compliance Through Insistence. You can regain control by attaching a drag leash to your dog. If he doesn't bring the ball back after you throw it, repeat your request and use the drag leash to enforce your command. The technique for using the drag leash is just like the one used for enforcing the *come* command. (See "Compliance Through Insistence for *Come* Defiance"). If your dog will not give up the ball once the drag leash is removed after working with it or if he becomes intermittent about giving you the ball, then you need to up the stakes and move on to Step 3, which combines time-outs and bartering.

Upping the Stakes

Start the session by first giving your dog a chance to come when you call and relinquish the toy. If he refuses, again use the drag leash to enforce your command, but only do this once. The second time your command goes unheeded, reel your dog in, then put him in his crate. After half an

119

If Your Dog Complains

If your dog begins to bark, yip, whine, or complain while in the crate, ignore him. Do not reprimand him. You are trying to teach the lesson that if he doesn't relinquish the ball, he is going to miss out. Don't confuse him by trying to make him be quiet. The more you ignore your dog, the more you'll drive home the point that you are in charge.

hour, take him out of the crate and again throw the ball. If he refuses to relinquish the ball, once again use the drag leash and immediately return him to the crate. Leave your dog there for up to an hour if possible. This time, when you take your dog out, do not go back to the game of tossing the ball. By ending your lesson at this point, you've given him something to think about. With a dog who has had a lot of practice not complying or with a dog who is highly invested in keeping control, you'll have more work before you see reform.

There are several aspects of this kind of training that will help turn your dog around. One is that you're stopping the playtime, which communicates to your dog that you are in control. You're then setting up a barter situation by letting him have a second chance to play, but only on your terms. If your dog fails to comply at that point, you've given him a chance to think over the consequences of not complying. Your next few lessons will be identical to your first lesson.

Success often comes by repeating this lesson several times until the dog decides to comply. Some dogs will give up after a few lessons only to again try things their way later. This isn't necessarily a bad thing—some dogs need to make at least one more attempt to take charge before they decide to let you be the boss. By keeping the consequences consistent, many dogs will give up trying to control the playtime.

Upping the Stakes Again—Playing "Hardball"

Some dogs are very stubborn or are very committed to doing things their way—or perhaps a little of both. For those dogs, you may have to play "hardball." I save this technique for my more difficult cases. If a dog still refuses to comply after having had multiple chances to do so, I find a way to make him miss out on playing when he decides not to relinquish the ball when told to.

The very first time your dog doesn't comply with your request to drop the ball, put him into the crate (as we did earlier), but add a step. Enlist the help of another dog, and start playing ball with him while your dog has to stay in the crate and watch. (You will need to do a little planning and arrange to have another dog handy.)

After a short time of playing with another dog, take your dog out of the crate and give him another chance to play and relinquish the ball. If he refuses, he goes back in the crate. Do this one or two more times so that your dog has a fair chance to decide to

Bonding Can Make a Difference for Compliance

Dogs who are independent or stubborn often see more reward in pleasing themselves. Although bonding can break through and reshape that kind of attitude, the right type of bonding is needed. A dog can easily show affection for his owner but not even consider obeying a command because he doesn't see his owner as the leader. Even when an owner offers praise, the value of such praise is diminished when the dog doesn't look up to him.

As discussed previously, there are several kinds of bonding. When it comes to compliance, dogs who are more dominant want to comply more with an owner they see as a worthy leader, whereas dogs who are more assertive may tend to bond with someone they see as part of the team. Unfortunately, if you are having compliance issues, bonding will suffer, which puts you in a situation where you are chasing your own tail. For your dog to see you as a strong leader/team player, you must get him to comply, but to get him to comply, he must see you as a strong leader/team player.

The best way I have found to break the noncompliance cycle is to work on the smaller issues and gain compliance there, such as the play issues we dealt with in this chapter. When you get compliance with the basics, you can often gain compliance in the more difficult areas. You will often find that once your dog accepts the idea, compliance will create more compliance. That is the kind of cycle you want.

comply on your terms. Each time your dog does relinquish the ball, praise him. The one time he doesn't, back in the crate he goes. Try to arrange to end the session on a positive note, with your dog doing as he is told.

Isn't This Kind of Training Teasing?

The previous exercise may seem like taunting or teasing. However, there are two things to keep in mind. First, your dog needs to understand that you're in charge of the play. He must learn to abide by your decision of how long and when he can play. That's what being in charge is all about. Second, because you've offered your dog an opportunity to earn his play by doing it on your terms, you're not teasing or taunting him. Teasing and taunting would be dangling something in front of him and then snatching it away, without ever giving him a chance to get what he wants.

Training by Trait

Part Three

Chapter Seven

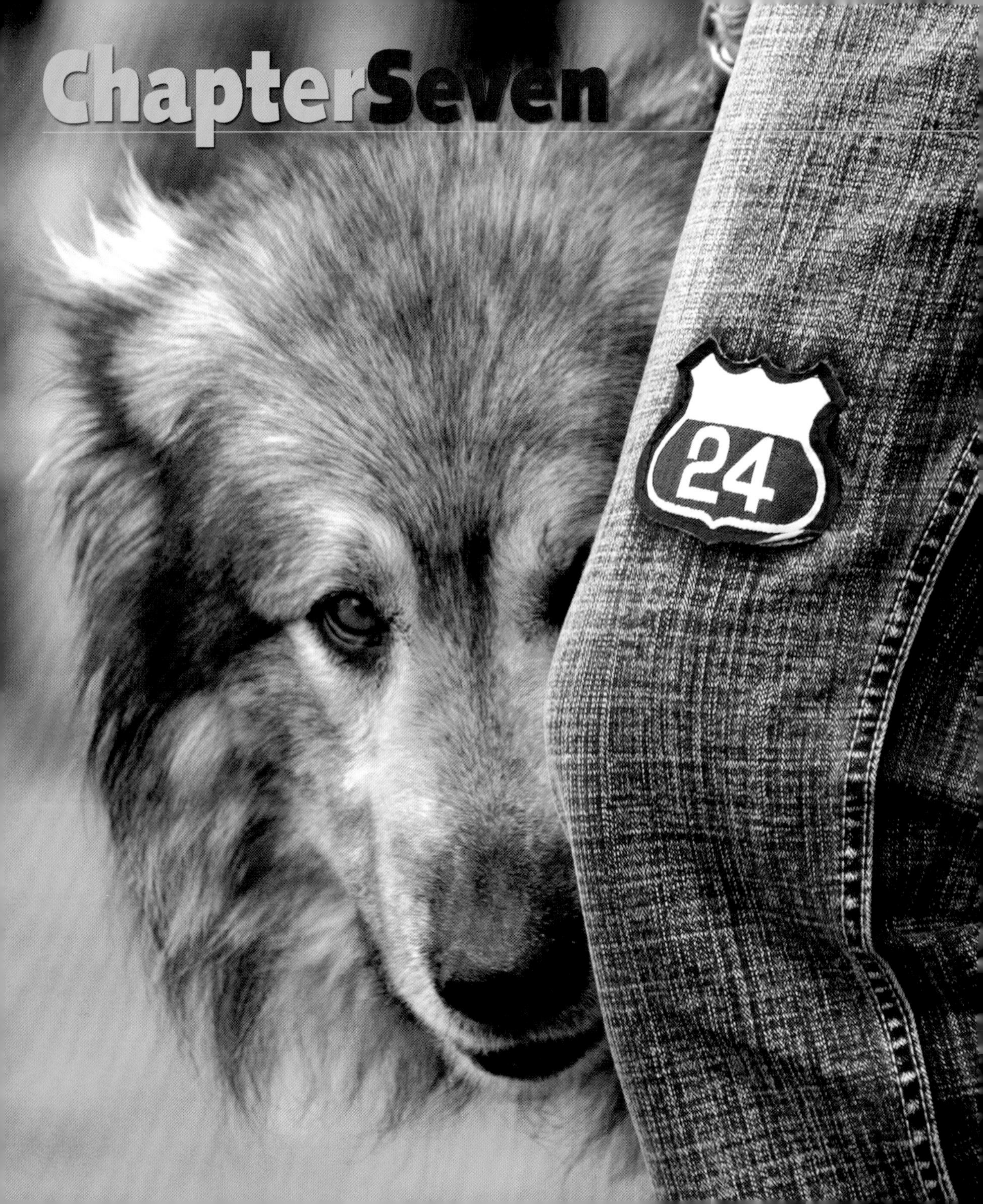

Training Group One Dogs:

Controlling the Controlling Dogs

The drive to take control is bred into dogs with dominant or assertive natures. Dogs of higher pack status also naturally want to take charge. In addition, a more independent nature creates a dog who wants to be in charge of himself. Dogs with a strong drive to take control need basic and power training to build a good foundation. (See Chapters 4 and 5.) However, additional training may be needed to help manage controlling canine behavior. It's essential to use the right type of training with these dogs because using the wrong techniques can cause avoidance behavior and destroy bonding.

Training Dominant Dogs

A dominant dog has a natural drive to seek more power, which makes taking charge something that comes easily to him. Problems occur when owners either don't train a more dominant dog or don't completely train him. Sometimes, owners stop at basic training, happy that their dog will sit and lie down on command—but for a dominant dog, this isn't enough.

Owners of dominant dogs must do the basic training in Chapter 4 and power training in Chapter 5. This training will help reinforce your leadership and show you how to control the issues of which a strong leader takes charge, including sleeping areas, food, attention, and playtime. If you fail to take charge in the areas a leader needs to control, your dog will take over.

Some people worry that their dog "won't like them" if they step into a strong leadership role. This can happen if harsh punishment is used to enforce your commands. However, if you use good training techniques, you'll form a strong bond with your dog. Also, it isn't unusual for some dominant dogs to also be very sensitive, making any kind of harsh training a poor choice. Persistence,

Persistence, insistence, and consistency work best when training a more dominant dog.

insistence, and consistency in training are what work best.

A dominant dog, especially one who is higher in pack status, may need reminders that you are in charge. You can do this by occasionally practicing his obedience training. You might want to incorporate this into a daily activity, such as when you feed him. Have him either sit or lie down, then require him to look at you and wait for a release to get his food. This will help serve as a reminder that you are the leader.

Independent Dogs

The dominance trait tends to lend itself toward a more independent nature. The independent dog thinks about serving himself and not his owner. These dogs do not have a natural drive to look toward anyone as a leader. The idea of doing anything other than their own wishes does not come natural to independent dogs, making training all the more important.

Basic training and power training will help teach an independent dog that he must interact with you and comply with your requests. Because the independent dog by nature doesn't think to look to a leader for any kind of guidance, training the *watch* command (see Chapter 4) is imperative.

When training the independent dog, don't force compliance. Arrange your training so that your dog learns to choose to comply. For example, pushing down his behind to get him to sit doesn't work well for the independent dog. Offering a reward when

Control May Be a Lifelong Pursuit

With some dogs, being in control is so important to them that trying to control them is a lifelong pursuit. There will be times when a controlling dog obeys not because he sees you as the ultimate one in control but because you've taught him that compliance is the only avenue you've left him to get the reward he wants. This kind of dog may never see you as the boss, but he may choose to do your bidding over his own if he becomes strongly bonded to you.

he chooses to sit on command is a better way to train.

Because independent dogs often have less interest in doing their owners' bidding, they may become quickly distracted during training sessions. Shorter training sessions can help, as can making sure that the reward is something in which the dog is very interested. Some independent dogs will prefer playing over treats as a reward. It can take some trial and error to discover what works with your dog and what doesn't. Training to gradually extend his attention span for tasks he deems uninteresting will also help with an independent dog.

Reclaiming Leadership

If you are having compliance issues with a more dominant or independent dog, he may not see you as a leader. To reclaim leadership, try adopting the following behaviors:

- *Don't step around your dog.* If your dog is in your way, ask him to move. A dog with control issues will want you to move out of his way. By insisting that he move, you are reinforcing your higher pack status.
- *Never give in to begging.* Ask your dog to follow a command or do a trick to earn every bite he gets from you. Ask him for a *sit-stay* while you put down his food bowl, and don't let him go to the food until you give a release word. The leader controls the food.
- *Control where your dog sleeps.* If he constantly challenges your authority, move where he sleeps every few nights. If you are having control issues, don't let him sleep in your bed.
- *Make your dog walk beside or behind you.* Walking ahead of you is not necessarily a dominance issue—some dogs walk ahead because they are excited or enthusiastic, or they may just be in the habit of pulling ahead. But if you are having control issues with your dog, you'll want to change this habit and have him follow behind or heel alongside of you.
- *Take control of play.* If you have a dog who is pesky or insistent about playing, you need to decide when it is time to play. If he prompts you to play by bringing a toy, ask him for a *sit* before you begin the play. Don't leave toys lying around. Keep them picked up and somewhere your dog can't get them. He must respect that you control these objects.

Teach your dog to walk beside you; if he's lunging ahead, you've lost control of him.

- *Don't give in to demands for attention.* Dogs who demand petting are often doing so because they feel in charge. There are, of course, exceptions. Golden Retrievers will often demand petting whether they see you as a leader or not—that trait just seems ingrained in the breed. However, a Golden Retriever who tips his head back and demands to be petted under the chin may be making a power move.

Only pet this kind of dog on the top of the head, and if you are having behavior issues, make sure that he earns his attention.

Ken and Cookie: Training a More Dominant Dog

Many people feel that problems with a particular dog may be due solely to dominance. But even in more dominant breeds, some individuals are easier to train than others, depending on other traits they may have. Two traits that make training a dominant dog more difficult are the dog's degree of independence and self-importance. The example of Ken and Cookie shows how to have success when working to get compliance from a tougher more dominant individual dog.

Cookie Wouldn't Listen to Ken

Cookie is my 11-inch, 12-pound (28-cm, 5-kg) Jack Russell Terrier. As far as her basic personality, she is higher in pack status, extremely strong willed, and on a scale of one to ten, about an eight in stubbornness. Like many Jack Russells, she is very independent, so the moment I step outside the house, she is content to take off in her own direction and pursue her own mission. I constantly need to work to keep her attention on me or on things I want her to do. Her higher degree of self-importance makes her often question why she should do my bidding over her own, and her stubborn nature drives her to resist my insistence that I should be in charge. (Chapter 8 talks more

about dealing with a stubborn nature.)

Because I worked with Cookie to train her for obedience and agility competitions, she eventually came to accept that she had to do what I told her. However, when it came to my 6-foot-tall (2-m) husband, Ken, Cookie was reluctant to do anything he asked. To

You can use a natural behavior your dog displays, like jumping up, to help with training.

129

get some kind of compliance, Ken would hold out a treat and ask for a *sit*. Cookie quickly decided that she would only comply if Ken first showed her the reward—which equates to treat blackmail (an issue covered in Chapter 5). To achieve more compliance, Ken attempted to bond with Cookie. When I was away teaching dog-training classes, Ken would coax Cookie up on the couch and pet her while she lay beside him. After several months, Cookie warmed up to Ken a little more, but she still had little interest in obeying any of his commands.

The Pancake Plan

Ken then took a different direction. When he made pancakes on the weekend, he noticed that Cookie was right by his side, waiting for him to toss her a little piece. One day, instead of tossing her a piece, he held it out over her head. She jumped up to try to get that desired treat, but instead of just giving it to her, Ken rotated the pancake in a large circle and said, "Dance." Because this "dance" behavior was very close to Cookie's natural behavior when offered a pancake (jumping up), it was easy for her to comply and get the reward. If Ken had tried a *sit* command, it would not have worked as well or so quickly because of Cookie's more stubborn nature. With stubborn dogs, you must start with a behavior they are already willing to do.

In no time at all, Cookie would dance on command for that pancake—even before Ken showed her the reward. She danced with more enthusiasm than anything she

Dancing on command for a treat comes easily to some dogs.

did for me and seemed to really enjoy it. I believe that she liked to dance because it was so close to a behavior she had already decided to offer to secure that treat.

Power Training

With more pieces of pancake in hand and the dance behavior done on command alone, Ken began to ask for more. He asked Cookie to sit for a pancake, which she did with more enthusiasm than for a regular dog biscuit, seeming to build on the enthusiasm from her dancing gig. Ken then went onto do some power training. (See Chapter 5.) This is where his relationship changed with Cookie. She learned to lie down and wait while Ken set down a piece of pancake and to stay put until he gave her a release word. Once she got that routine down, he began to ask Cookie to look at him before he gave her a release word.

Because pancakes were a weekly event, Ken practiced consistently with Cookie, which brought about a profound change in her relationship with him. Cookie began to obey all the commands Ken told her without looking to see if he had a dog biscuit as a reward. She also changed in how affectionate she was toward him. Before the power training, Cookie was indifferent; after the power training, she became more bonded to Ken. When he came home from work, Cookie began to whine and fuss in anticipation of seeing him. Before, she would hardly lift her head off the couch when she heard him pull into the garage. The power training had formed a stronger bond than just sitting and petting her on the couch had done.

Agility can provide much-needed mental and physical stimulation for an assertive dog.

Dominant dogs, independent dogs, and even those with a high degree of self-importance seem to grow closer to their owners when they deem their owner a worthy leader. However, the more independent and full of self-importance your dog is, the more you will need to remind him to look to you for guidance. Ken still goes though his training routine with Cookie each time he makes pancakes, which is typically at least once a week.

Assertive Dogs

Although some people consider the dominant dog the most difficult to deal with, I consider the assertive trait the most challenging. The assertive dog has a quick mind that tries to come up with a better idea on how to do anything and everything. Even if you have established yourself as leader, an assertive dog will persist in trying things his way. Because this type of dog often has seemingly endless energy, he can wear out an owner who isn't using him for the job he was bred for (such as herding or getting an animal to bolt from a den). The assertive dog is hardwired to take charge over an animal, and lacking that opportunity, will work endlessly to take charge of his owner.

Highly assertive dogs need both physical and mental exercise. If you own this kind of dog and don't offer him the opportunity to use his assertive nature, you may find him practicing on you. Although obedience training and power training help, unless you allow your dog to exhaust his mental and physical energies, you will find yourself challenged by his assertive nature. Using the *watch* command with an assertive dog has great benefits, so consider having him make eye contact and wait for a release command at mealtimes. However, to convince your dog that he needs to choose your way over his, you must train him to see you as part of his team.

Harsh training methods don't work—pain or physical punishment will not deter many highly assertive dogs from their mission. These dogs were bred to do their job in spite of pain or punishment, creating a dog who will work endlessly until he gets his way and not necessarily be detoured by punishment. One of the best ways to get compliance from this kind of dog is to strongly bond with him. Using harsh reprimands or dominating techniques can work against bonding with a dog.

With an assertive dog, you will find that the training isn't a final event. Sure, these dogs are very quick learners; however, you will need to give him reminders that he needs to comply with your requests.

Endless Energy Issues

Many assertive dogs have high-energy demands. In general, dogs who don't get enough exercise are prone to problem behaviors, but the assertive dog will tend to become even more assertive and demanding, as it's one way to vent excess energy. Unfortunately, even a mile (km) or two a day aren't enough for these dogs—some will have enough energy to go all day long without any desire to lounge in the sunshine for a nap. Few people have time to spend making sure that their dogs get enough of a workout. Even runners who take their dogs on a run for several miles (km) may find that after a few hours of rest, they are ready to go again.

More than miles (km) are required to wear out these dogs. They need physical and mental challenges because they've been bred to have endurance as well as to match wits with another animal. When an assertive dog doesn't have mental challenges, he may turn his efforts toward taking control of his owner.

By offering your dog a mental challenge, you will find that he wears out faster than just by exercising alone. Play sessions with your dog can be a great way to vent excess energy and stimulate his mind, and they have the added benefit of helping him bond with you.

Many dogs find digging to be a self-rewarding behavior.

Jack and His Working Border Collie

Jack took up the hobby of competing with his Border Collie in sheep herding trials. One day, while discussing how assertive this breed could be about doing things its own way, Jack told me that he and his dog approached the sheep herding competition as a team. He recalled how, during one competition, he'd given his dog a command. There was a brief moment when Jack noticed that his dog hesitated and debated doing what he was told but then complied. It turns out that Jack had given his dog the wrong command, and they lost the competition.

The Border Collie was seasoned enough to know that the command was wrong, and he very much wanted to do things his own way. However, because the two were bonded through their teamwork, he decided to comply with Jack's incorrect command. They may have lost, but they lost as a team—their strong bond meant the dog would comply no matter what.

Self-Rewarding Behavior

One of the biggest problems with some of the higher-energy assertive dogs is that their clever minds seldom rest. If they don't get enough physical and mental challenges, they'll come up with their own. The challenging part of these unwanted behaviors is that they are self-rewarding. Take for instance chasing a horse, an activity many assertive dogs truly love. There is no treat tasty enough to lure the dog from the chase. Not even a kick from the horse will deter most of these dogs. Because the dog finds reward in the behavior, he has little incentive to change. Part of the solution is to find a way of sabotaging the reward in the behavior and

to work to redirect the dog toward a more acceptable behavior. Keep in mind that these dogs often act out because they have excess energy that needs venting, so another part of the solution involves increasing their playtime or finding an acceptable job for them to do.

Avoidance Behavior

Many assertive dogs have a high degree of avoidance behavior—their quick minds have learned how to use this trait well. Unfortunately, these dogs never seem to avoid the behaviors we want them to. If you correct a dog with a highly-refined avoidance behavior, he won't necessarily decide to stop the action that caused the correction. Instead, he'll figure out how to continue the action and prevent the correction. This is a trait bred into many herding type dogs, and it's a good reason to avoid using harsh punishment because the dog will persist in the misbehavior no matter what.

The Role of Bonding

Bonding is a driving factor in compliance. However, there are different ways in which a dog will bond with a person, and the strongest bonds will be associated with the dog's basic drives. One kind of bonding is affection bonding. Some breeds and some individual dogs seem to have a strong need for affection and will readily bond when it is offered. Many Labrador and Golden Retrievers, for example, will accept affection from almost any human who is willing to pet them. These dogs even cherish affection from owners who show poor leadership.

Another kind of bonding comes from strong leadership. In this chapter, we saw how strong leadership helped forge a bond between Ken and Cookie. Often, the more dominant breeds will also favor this kind of bonding. Rottweilers and Bulldogs typically

A combination of affection and strong leadership can help you bond with a more dominant dog.

want to bond more strongly with people who show good leadership over people who merely show them affection. With this kind of bonding, the better you control the resources, the more your dog will see you as the leader and the stronger he will bond to you. However, this kind of bond will be weakened if you show poor or inconsistent leadership. Likewise, if you are constantly using harsh techniques to maintain control of your dog, the bond will become damaged.

Dogs will also bond if they see you as a team player. Assertive dogs favor this kind of bond, especially when they are allowed to work with their owners doing what they were bred for. Other activities that strengthen this kind of bond include taking a dog for a walk or a run or playing with him.

Bartering to Change Unwanted Behaviors

Owners of assertive dogs may need to learn how to barter with their dogs for compliance. In some ways, you barter when training with treats—you show your dog a treat and ask for a command. He understands that to get the treat (what he wants) he must do the command (what you want). This is the basics of bartering.

Bartering causes some owners to worry that they aren't in complete control of their dog, so therefore it's not the best way to train. After all, you are not forcing the dog to do what you ask but arranging for him to choose to do what you ask. However, with an assertive dog bred to take charge in a working situation, it is in his nature to make

Don't force an assertive dog to comply— try the bartering method instead.

choices. Forcing him to comply will only lead to problems. Bartering, when done well, can work to convince a dog to choose to comply.

How to Barter With Your Dog

To barter, you must offer your dog something he really wants. Treats work well with training food-motivated dogs, and play can be used in a similar manner. If your dog is more hardwired to please, then praise can typically motivate him to comply. Unfortunately, for some dogs there is more motivation in doing things their way than there is in treats or praise. For these dogs, a different barter system is needed.

To barter with a dog who isn't food or praise motivated, you must set up a controlled training situation and create an activity he likes to do. Then you must prevent him from doing what he wants unless he chooses to comply.

For bartering to work, you need to control the situation so that your dog has something to gain by complying. When you use this kind of barter, often the reward is that the dog gets to participate in an action he wants to do rather than losing the privilege of participation. Trying to set up a successful barter with a dog often takes persistence and creativity.

An Example of Bartering on an Agility Course

Border Collies predominate on agility courses. These dogs are fast and very dedicated to work—they are the workaholics of the dog world. Repetition doesn't bother them as long as they are actively engaged in a mission. Unfortunately, a clash of wills can occur on the agility course because Border Collies are also bred to engage their intellect while they work. They were bred to make moment-by-moment decisions to outsmart sheep while herding. Out on the agility course, there are no animals to control, so some Border Collies want to take charge of the decisions made when running it. This results in them doing obstacles without waiting for their owners' commands.

Because running agility is a team effort, punishment can't be used when handler and dog have a clash of wills. Punishment would only destroy the teamwork and bonding between dog and handler. However,

A Border Collie may want to take charge of the decisions on an agility course.

without some kind of consequences, there is no incentive for the dog to choose to follow his handler's commands over the way he has decided to do things. To enforce compliance, many Border Collie handlers will stop the run and remove the dog from the course if he's not following commands. It's a form of barter—for the dog to get what he wants (running the course), then he must do what the handler wants (wait for and follow commands). Using this kind of technique puts the dog owner back in control and achieves compliance without using a destructive force such as punishment.

Be Careful When Using a Drag Leash

Although I've mentioned it before, it warrants repeating—never use a drag leash to catch your dog and then correct him. Entrapment of this sort with harsh punishment can create a neurosis or overly submissive behavior. Just the act of stopping the misbehaving dog is enough. Also, don't leave a drag leash on your dog when you can't watch him. Dogs can get tangled or hurt themselves if you aren't around to intervene.

Twinkie Was Independent, Assertive, and Quite Happy not Complying

Twinkie, a rescued mix, is a good example of a dog who has a combination of several traits in this group that made her a hard-to-train dog. Dale, Twinkie's owner, ran into a problem when she was about a year old. Dale would spend time outside training his dog and then would engage in a play session afterward. The problem started when it was time to go inside. Dale would call Twinkie, but she would sit on the grass in a sunny spot and just stare at him. When he took the leash out of his pocket to catch her, she would run (avoidance behavior) and make a game out of getting caught (reward for her misbehavior). Finally, Dale began hiding the leash in his pocket and would approach Twinkie with a treat to catch her, but what he really wanted was for her to come inside when she was called.

For Dale to achieve his goal, he had to resolve several issues. First, he needed to break Twinkie's bad habit of avoiding being caught when she didn't want to comply. Then, he needed to train his dog to come when called, even if she didn't want to. To do this, he had to create a habit of compliance. There are many ways to approach this, but in Dale's situation, the easiest way was to take the reward out of disobeying and put it back into obeying.

Step One: Take Control and Establish Your Leadership

Twinkie needed to see Dale as more of a leader. Dale needed to insist on compliance (see Chapter 6) with Twinkie by teaching her to let him catch her when he wanted. He began by attaching a drag leash to Twinkie's collar before they went outside. The drag leash served two purposes. First, if Dale came over to catch Twinkie and she tried to dash off, he could stop her by stepping on the drag leash. This taught Twinkie that she couldn't run off. Second, the drag leash could be used to enforce the *come* command. When Dale called Twinkie to come and she didn't obey, he could pick up the end of the leash and pull her to him. (He didn't jerk the leash but used it to guide Twinkie back to him.) Dale then petted, praised, and treated Twinkie, even though he had to use the leash to pull her over when he said "Come." This helped reinforce Dale as the leader (because she wasn't allowed to disobey), as well as reinforce the idea that there is a reward for compliance.

Step Two: Make the Come Command a Reward

Funnily enough, it was Dale who accidentally taught Twinkie not to come! Because he called her to come right after outdoor playtime and the fun typically ended after she came when called, Dale ended up removing the reward for coming. Twinkie figured that if she didn't come, the fun could continue. Dale reinforced her hypothesis by chasing her to catch her. Twinkie, being a rather creative dog, quickly realized that the chase game was a new kind of fun.

Bartering and bonding are two valuable tools for dealing with a controlling dog.

Dale needed to make compliance rewarding by changing the *come* command into a fun game. Because Twinkie loved to play, especially with a squeaky toy, he decided to use it to make *come* fun for her. Dale began by calling out the *come* command, and immediately afterward, he took out the toy and started squeaking it. When Twinkie arrived, Dale took a few moments to play with her. After a while, when Dale called for Twinkie to come, she'd start to respond before he even used the squeaky toy. At this point, Dale waited until she arrived to take out the toy and play with it. In addition, when Dale did need to call her inside for the day, he rewarded her for compliance by taking a moment to play with her inside the house. After Twinkie got in the habit of coming when called, Dale started to fade the reward. However, for quite some time after the new habit was developed, he did some intermittent reinforcement for compliance with play or a tasty treat.

Although many dominant dogs will learn how to comply from power training and strong leadership, when dealing with an assertive dog, you must employ some specialized techniques to gain compliance. Two of the most valuable tools you can use are bartering and bonding. Bartering helps you achieve compliance without precipitating avoidance behavior. Bonding will help encourage your dog to choose to comply over giving in to his urge to do things his way.

Chapter Eight

Training Group Two Dogs:

Gaining Compliance With "Stubborn As a Mule" Dogs

Issues with stubbornness or intermittent compliance can start out simple, such as the Boxer who plants all fours and refuses to move, or the Shiba Inu who ignores your command, or just about any behavior in the wide world of terriers. When dealing with a dog who has a stubborn nature, you must figure out a way to get him to comply without using force. By using the right techniques, you can find a way to solicit cooperation while avoiding drawing out the stubborn tendencies of the dog.

As Stubborn as a Mule

When you think of the word "stubborn," do you picture a terrier? How about a mule? Brad Cameron is a renowned mule trainer, and I learned a lot about training stubborn dogs from his experience with mules.

According to Brad, "Mules are smart. They spend a lot of time thinking about what you are doing and trying to figure you out. Training takes a little longer with a mule. Not because they don't understand, but their compliance comes when they feel it is in their best interest and in their own time, not in ours. Mules will not be coerced, threatened, or forced. This goes for physical brutality or force through hardware of some kind. The way mules are made up, mentally, they want a friend.

"Unfortunately, too many people do not want to be the mule's friend, and they start out, through old standard training methods, to show him that the human is something to be feared. This creates great and sometimes insurmountable resistance in the mule (as it would with anything or anybody). There is a ridiculous old saying that if you are mean to a mule, he will wait to get even with you. Nothing could be farther from the truth! Mules cannot think on our terms, they are not vindictive, they do not plot against us, and they have no desire at all to get even. If a mule has been mistreated, he may simply find it more comfortable to keep humans away from him using the only defense he has—a kick.

"If you want to work with your mule in a better way, you have to see beyond the hair on his hide. There are a lot of people who cannot see past the hair and have no concept of the great possibilities that lie within. Take it from someone who was there once—there is a whole other world available once you begin to achieve true understanding.

"The training of the mule in this manner is really more of a philosophy than cut-and-dry training methods. To work with your mule, you are continually presenting something to him and asking him to follow your direction—presenting and asking, not forcing and telling. This is much like how you would present the idea of going on a trail ride to a friend and asking if he would like to go with you. By looking at things from the mule's point of view and presenting your program in a way that he can understand, you will not be building resistance. Instead, you will have a relationship with a friend for life."

I like to think of Brad's training as the "mule principle"—find a way to get the animal to choose to comply.

Training the Stubborn Dog Is Different

Your training techniques will make a difference in how your dog responds. For years, the popular way to train basic obedience was to force a dog to comply, which meant that his back end was shoved down into a *sit* or a choke collar was used. While not the best method, this harsher "do it my way or else" technique worked for some dogs. But a more strong-willed, independent dog may become as resistant as a mule with this approach. The best method is one that is reward based—ask for a task, then offer a reward for compliance. For example, as we learned in Chapter 4, teach your dog to sit by holding a treat over his nose and luring him into the *sit* position.

Sometimes Fixing a Stubborn Trait With Rewards Can Be Easy

With some dogs, breaking them away from a stubborn trait can be easier than

Some dogs, like Jack Russell Terriers, are notorious for planting all fours when learning to walk on a leash.

with others. Instead of reacting to the problem with force, react by setting up a reward for compliance.

If you have a puppy, it's essential to start rewarding for compliance right way because the younger the dog is, the better results you will have.

For example, some breeds are notorious for suddenly planting all fours when learning to walk on leash. The dog will simply plant his feet and refuse to go any farther. If your dog begins this behavior, keep some tasty treats in your pocket and try luring him with a treat when it happens. The first time, it may take a bit of time for your dog to move. You might end up rewarding him for the attempt to walk to you and not for perfect compliance. But the second time, you'll probably get a few steps forward. Your dog still may attempt the behavior a few more times, but he should lure out of the refusal more quickly. Finally, your dog should abandon the behavior.

Sometimes Fixing a Stubborn Trait With Rewards Isn't so Easy

While force definitely doesn't work, some dogs won't be coaxed into compliance with a treat. With this type of a dog, you'll have to limit his options for misbehaving and work extra hard to make compliance the most logical choice. Let's look at an example of this technique with a noncompliant Lhasa Apso.

A Lhasa Apso who was learning to jump in an agility class succeeded in jumping once or twice for a treat, then decided that

Agility Training Techniques

Dogs trained for agility need a very high level of compliance. Even if you never plan to participate in agility, there are many techniques discovered by agility dog trainers that can help pet owners. Try taking a basic agility class, or read up on agility training methods.

it was much easier to go around the jump. The Lhasa's owner responded by attaching a leash and dragging her dog over jumps. Like many harsher methods, this is not the best way to train. The Lhasa Apso reacted to being dragged over jumps much like a mule—it made him more reluctant than when he began.

To resolve the problem, the Lhasa's owner tried a different technique. She was instructed to hold out the reward on one side of the jump. A dog handler took the dog to the other side of the jump and directed him toward it. The dog handler used her hands to herd the dog toward the obstacle, tightening up when he tried to escape and letting loose when he focused on the task. The small dog was not forced to jump, but neither was he allowed to go around the jump. Because the option of running around the jump was eliminated, the Lhasa decided to jump and was immediately rewarded on the other side. The dog then took the next jump without hesitation. Lesson learned: Allowing your dog to make the decision to cooperate

creates a willing dog; forcing him creates a reluctant, more stubborn dog.

Training Stubborn Puppies

Katie, a black and white rough-coated Jack Russell Terrier, was only eight weeks old when her stubborn streak reared its ugly head. We had the good fortune of studying the consequences of certain behavior modification with her because Katie was one of five puppies in a litter my daughter raised.

Right away, Katie put the pursuit of her own wishes over that of the rest of

Working with a young puppy to reform a stubborn streak will help get more compliance as an adult.

Show your puppy there is reward in compliance.

the puppies. She would often stop on a walk and refuse to keep up with her littermates. She wasn't distracted when she stopped—she just sat down and refused to keep up. She wanted the world to bend to her will. Of course, we didn't. We kept going and encouraged her to again join the procession.

We were concerned to see such a high degree of stubbornness at such an early age. Katie persisted in lingering whenever she was called. Things finally came to a climax one day right after she was let inside the house. The rest of the puppies had followed along as we coaxed them to go into their pen, but Katie sat down a short distance inside the doorway and refused to budge. In response, I went over and made

my invitation more personalized by calling her name in a happy and excited voice and clapping and coaxing her. Katie sat with a self-righteous stare. Food didn't impress her—we stuck cheese right in front of her face to try to lure her, and it didn't work. She had planted her bottom and was not going to comply.

We knew that she loved playtime, so I got out a squeak toy and tried to lure Katie with it. The pup fidgeted a little but then decided that she was not going to move. At that point, I was tempted to grab her and drag her to her place, thereby making her comply with my command, but I didn't. There is so much more of an advantage if the dog makes the decision to comply on his own. I wanted to try one more thing.

We took all the puppies a short distance away and again called for Katie to come. She remained firmly planted. I then started playing with the other puppies, making sure that between the sound of squeaky toys and my happy-sounding voice that Katie knew that we were all having a lot of fun. Finally, Katie joined us and was immediately rewarded with play.

The next time Katie decided to sit and be stubborn, I only called once and then went to the task of playing excitedly with another puppy. One thing a high-drive dog like a Jack Russell Terrier can't stand is to be left out of whatever is going on—especially if it sounds like fun. This time, Katie took even less time to give in and join the play. My daughter and I realized that we were on to something and kept chipping away at Katie's stubborn streak. We made sure that she knew she was missing out on something fun, and we played with her a little extra when she did decide to comply.

At four months of age, Katie went to a new home. We touched base with her owner a year later, who commented that Katie wasn't as stubborn as the other Jack Russells he'd owned and was amazingly cooperative. It helped, I suspect, that we were able to work with Katie when she was so young to help reform her stubborn streak.

Your goal is to create a habit of compliance with a stubborn dog.

Sabotaging a Puppy's Stubborn Streak

The most effective way to sabotage a stubborn streak is to set up a training situation in which the dog learns that the reward is in the compliance. The sooner he chooses to comply, the sooner he gets a reward. If you try to force your dog to comply, you may create even more stubbornness, or he may take up the challenge to figure out a way to get that reward without complying. In Katie's situation, she learned that being stubborn meant that she would miss out on fun things. By using a strong motivator, Katie learned that being stubborn was not as rewarding as compliance.

Training Stubborn Adults

Pollyanna and Molly, four-year-old Pomeranians, had rough lives before Verna adopted them. Both were used as breeding bitches in a puppy mill. Neither had proper training, and Pollyanna had lost her eye to abuse. Even though Verna gave the dogs a lot of love, Pollyanna needed a little help when it came to following requests because out of the two, she had a very stubborn nature. If you asked Pollyanna to take a single step in your direction, she'd stubbornly refuse. People typically had to go over to her and pick her up.

I kept Pollyanna for about a week when she was ten years old. To get her over her resistance to going into her pen when asked, I used some tasty dog treats. I held out the dog treat, but Pollyanna held her ground.

Clicker Training

Some people find that using clicker training helps when working with a stubborn dog. The clicker can be used to shape wanted behavior and seems to engage a dog's mind in favor of the command you are trying to get him to do. Check out the resources section for information on clicker training.

After five minutes of coaxing, Pollyanna took one step toward the pen. Although the step was the result of her deciding to move for another reason, I praised and rewarded her. The next day, she tried the step thing a little sooner—after all, I was holding out her favorite treat. Again, she received praise and a reward. The next day, Pollyanna lured all the way into the pen. After that, getting her to go into her pen was quite simple. She needed time to think through complying with my request, and she needed a lot of encouragement. Once she discovered that compliance brought reward, Pollyanna became more willing to cooperate.

The lesson I taught Pollyanna was that there is reward in compliance. Although she hardly complied the first night, she did find reward in a behavior other than stubbornly refusing. I stopped the lesson there because she needed to think things over. Because I had already had some experience working with stubborn dogs, I didn't know if the next lesson would bring more resistance or if she would decide to give in a little more. Luckily, it was the latter. I stopped the lesson after each small success because there is a great advantage in ending positively rather than pushing to the point where the dog again becomes resistant. Although Pollyanna may have been willing to do more than what I had asked in that second lesson, I didn't want to chance losing ground with her reform, so I ended after one success. I admit that I was a little surprised that after the third night, Pollyanna seemed to not care about resisting any more and was quite content to focus on the reward—but then, she did love her "Pup-peroni" treats.

Reforming Stubborn Adults

When working with adult dogs who are in a routine of noncompliance, a lot of work is involved in their reform. However, the basic "mule principle" still works—you must let the animal choose to comply. But be aware that many of these dogs will automatically default to trying to outsmart and manipulate you when you ask for a task, and they may be dedicated to finding a way to get what they want without having to comply.

To reform a stubborn dog, you must:

- Create a habit of compliance. (Obedience training is a great foundation.)
- Let your dog learn that the quickest way to get what he wants is to comply.

Once your dog learns the secret to getting what he wants—doing your bidding—training other tasks typically become easier.

Work From Simple to Complex

When asking for your dog's cooperation, work from simple to more complex. If you have a dog who absolutely refuses to do anything you ask, you'll have to show him that there is a reward for compliance. Find something he does naturally, and offer a reward. Let's say that you have a dog who likes to jump up. When he jumps up on his own, say a word like "Up," then give a treat. After a few times of rewarding him for jumping on his own, hold out a treat and say "Up." When he performs the task in response to your command, give a

When working with a stubborn dog, capture a natural behavior he offers and reward it.

Stubborness combined with oversensitivity makes for a very challenging dog.

reward. If your dog paws at you when he wants something, say "Paw," then hold out something he will most likely paw to get. When your dog paws, say "Good paw." If he comes running when he hears the can opener, call out "Come" just before you open his can of food. Capturing these natural behaviors is the first step in teaching your dog that there is a reward for compliance.

When you are rewarding the behavior your dog does naturally, maintain control over the reward and the behavior. Once your dog understands the *up* command, don't give any reward for this action unless you requested it. Otherwise, he will use the task to demand a treat. If your dog paws at you when you

didn't ask, tell him "No" and walk away. Later, get a treat, say "Paw," and then reward him when he does it on command. During the teaching phase, you can reward for offered behaviors, but once your dog learns the command, he must understand that the reward is only given for compliance.

Intermittent Compliance

Lestat, a Jack Russell Terrier, was a master of all the agility equipment, and I even watched his former owner take him through a perfect run at top speed for a first-place ribbon. Unfortunately, he was also a master at intermittent compliance. Lestat decided that agility was boring, so he started making up his own course. The weave poles were the biggest problem, which he would do haphazardly or omit altogether. When scolded for expressing such creativity, Lestat—an overly sensitive dog—would shut down or become defiant, sometimes even leaving the course. Call him a stubborn dog or just one with compliance issues—either way, Lestat wasn't obeying commands he knew how to do.

Combination Traits

Stubbornness combined with oversensitivity makes for a very challenging dog. Using harsh punishment or corrections with these dogs creates negative issues and makes the original problem more difficult to resolve. The problem ends up taking on a life of its own, and corrections only create new problems. When this happens, it's typically due to more than one underlying cause, which means that one simple solution doesn't exist.

Lestat had several factors that fed his reluctance to comply. He was a social climber who was always on the lookout for an opportunity to advance his standing. He was also a terrier bred from a hunting line, which gave him an intense and assertive nature (yet another hard-to-train trait!). He loved to throw himself into everything he did, and when his handler wasn't fast enough

When it came to agility, Lestat wanted to run the show.

on the agility course, he gave himself license to make up his own course.

Setting a Goal for Retraining

The goal with Lestat's retraining was to get him to perform agility for his owner. Lestat had to learn that he couldn't pick and choose his obstacles; he had to be taught to do them correctly and not to leave the course. Because leaving the course was a direct result of Lestat's frustration over his owner's reprimands and disapproval, correcting the first two issues would help eliminate the last one.

The first step to Lestat's reform was to drop all reprimands. If Lestat did anything wrong, nothing negative was said or done. Not even a "no" was offered. Instead, the command for the obstacle was repeated and verbal encouragement offered for anything done right.

The second step was to work at home on jumps and his favorite issue, the weave poles. Lestat loved playing with a ball, so that's what was used as his reward. (Actually, he was obsessed with playing ball, but this terrier was very intense and very prone to obsessive/compulsive behaviors.)

Lestat was given a little playtime with the ball to sharpen his interest in the reward. While he was still interested in the play, he was asked to earn more playtime by taking a jump on command. Lestat acted as if he didn't understand the command and asked for the ball by jumping up and down. The ball was not thrown, but the command was repeated. Lestat still wouldn't jump, so he

Let Creative Dogs Try Doing Things Their Way First

Don't get angry at a dog who insists on using creativity to get his way. Be consistent and keep asking and rewarding compliance on your terms, even as he continues to try to do things his way. This will teach him that there is reward in compliance and no reward in doing things his way. With some dogs, this process will take a long time, at least at first. But soon he will get in the habit of accepting compliance for new tasks more quickly. The key is to let the dog make this choice, not force it.

was lured over the jump with the ball. After Lestat jumped, he received play as a reward, and the training session ended.

The next training session, Lestat was shown the ball and asked to jump. Again, he needed to be lured over the jump. The same process described earlier was repeated until the session ended.

Using a Crate for Retraining

During the next training session, Lestat was again asked to jump. He ignored the command and asked for the ball, still wanting to play on his terms. After Lestat ignored several encouragements to comply, he was put into a crate a few feet (m) away from the practice area.

Putting a dog into a crate is "upping the stakes" for compliance, as we discussed

151

in Chapter 6. This technique only works if the dog knows what he needs to do to get the reward, which is why in the previous sessions, Lestat was shown twice how to attain the reward.

After half an hour, Lestat was taken out of the crate and shown the ball. He was asked to jump, which he did. Lestat was then rewarded by playing with the ball. This is usually the turning point with many dogs. Lestat was allowed to choose to comply to get what he wanted. With some dogs, once they try getting their way and fail but find success through compliance, a major battle has been won. Once this happens, you can ask the dog to jump, reward with play, and then begin to ask for more commands. Eventually, you can completely fade the reward and substitute with praise.

Training Compliance Takes Time

Some dogs will not be reformed so easily. Factors that influence how easily a dog will reform include:

- how long he's been allowed to get his way
- how stubborn his nature is
- how high his pack status is
- if he sees you as a strong leader
- if lessons are daily or too much time elapses between sessions

Lestat wasn't ready to comply after one success. The next training session, he took the jump without being asked, then came running over for his reward, but a reward was not given. Instead, Lestat was again asked to jump on command. He refused.

If your dog's been allowed to get his way for a long time, his reform may take extra time.

He was put back in his crate for half an hour and again asked to comply. When Lestat did comply, he received playtime as a reward. After a few time-outs in the crate as a consequence of noncompliance, Lestat decided to give in. Once he became good at jumping one jump on command, another jump was added. After several jumps were done successfully on command, Lestat began working on weave poles using the same techniques as the jumps.

When dealing with a stubborn dog, expect to work hard to get compliance at first, see some backsliding, and finally get into the habit of compliance. These dogs take time to reform and may need to be reminded from time to time that they need to comply.

Formula for Success

While every stubborn dog's solution will be a little different, the basic formula for success is to find something your dog really wants and allow him to try to get it on his terms—but then make sure that he doesn't succeed. Then, show him how to get what he wants by doing what you ask. The first request should be something simple so that you can easily get your dog to comply. With persistence, he will finally conclude that the fastest way to get what he wants is to do what you want. Once your dog decides to give compliance a try, you can work toward more complex requests. Remember, although you need to be generous with rewards at first, don't quench your dog's appetite with too many treats or too much playtime. Always stop a training session before he is bored and while he is still interested in play or treats. This will keep his interest sharp and prevent boredom, which just invites problem behaviors.

With stubborn and strong-willed dogs, much like the mule, you can't force compliance. You must let your dog choose to comply by making compliance the best choice.

Stop the training session before your dog gets bored.

ChapterNine

Training Group Three Dogs:

Desensitizing "Nervous Nellies"

Shyness can arise on its own, or it can come bundled with other traits. Shy dogs can also be highly sensitive, highly reactive, or a combination both. These traits can create a dog who becomes rattled by loud noises, who stresses out when his owner is nervous or there is tension in the household, or who overreacts to corrections from his owner.

When a dog has all three traits—shyness, high reactivity, and high sensitivity—working to get him to function in a more stable manner not only demands some very creative techniques but can require constant reinforcement.

Shy Dogs

Shyness is a trait that makes owning and training a dog more difficult. Some dogs are shy because of their genetic makeup. Shyness can crop up in any breed; however, breeds such as Shetland Sheepdogs, Belgian Tervurens, and some of the terrier breeds—who have more reserved natures—are more likely to have shyer individuals. Dogs who are not adequately socialized also tend toward shyness. Although all dog owners need to socialize their dogs to prevent shyness issues, when dealing with a shyer dog, socialization can take specialized techniques and require an extensive time commitment.

Your Dog's Social Aptitude

Most of the training of a shy dog deals with socialization, which means introducing

Some dogs are outgoing and love meeting new people and other dogs.

Some dogs are reserved and prefer to meet strangers on their own terms.

Although dogs vary in their degree of stability, by deciding where your dog falls in these three main categories, you can better decide how to approach successful socialization. For simplicity, I've used the colors of a stoplight to help identify the major tendencies of different dogs.

Green for Go

A green dog acts as if all dogs and people have been waiting around for his arrival and the privilege of his company. This dog readily marches up to strange dogs and has no hesitation approaching people he's never met.

Socialization With the Green Dog

Green dogs take only a minimum amount of socializing. It's easy to socialize the green dog by attending puppy class and getting him around a few adults, children, and other dogs. However, a green dog who has little or no socialization may become reserved. Luckily, it only takes a little effort to socialize these types of dogs, even at an older age.

Yellow for Reserved

The yellow dog is reserved. He is willing to accept strangers and strange dogs but prefers to do so on his own terms. If a strange person or dog rushes up to a yellow dog, he will immediately back off. However, if you stop close to a reserved dog, he'll be more willing to approach you and make a quiet introduction. Once the yellow dog knows a person or dog, he will be

him to people and other dogs. Dogs who are not shy are usually comfortable with people and other dogs, and many of their socialization needs can be met by attending a puppy class. However, a shy or reserved dog will require much more socialization work. A shy dog must be carefully introduced to people and other dogs of different sizes, sexes, ages, and demeanors.

A good way to approach socializing your dog is to understand his social aptitude.

comfortable when he approaches. This dog can have a fairly large circle of people and dogs with whom he is comfortable, as long as the socialization proceeds at his pace and is not rushed.

Socialization With the Yellow Dog

The yellow dog requires more work than a green dog. Reserved dogs can become selectively social and may feel at ease with only certain kinds of people, such as women but not all men, or certain kinds of dogs, such as calm dogs but not excitable ones.

Taking a yellow dog to a puppy class is a great way to start the socialization process, but unlike the green dog, you'll typically need to do more work. Expose the yellow dog to many different types of people, including males who are large in stature, women, and children of different ages. Introduce the yellow dog to a variety of sizes and breeds, including some of the more powerful breeds, because these dogs can have a different demeanor. Yellow dogs must be socialized outside of puppy class because they may not transfer the confidence they gain in class to strange dogs they meet.

Some reserved dogs remain reserved all their lives. Others, with enough work, can socialize well enough so that they become more green than yellow. Although the younger the better for socialization, expect to continue to work with this type of dog for at least the first year of life and sometimes until he is two or three.

Some dogs are shy and will hold back in most situations.

Red for Shy

Red symbolizes the shy dog who will want to stop or hold back in most situations. These dogs can be dog shy, people shy, or both. A shy dog will not approach people he doesn't know and will flee either strange dogs or people who approach him. These dogs have a small circle of people and dogs with whom they are comfortable. The shyer the dog, the smaller his circle of comfort.

Socialization With the Red Dog

As hard as you try, you'll never turn a shy dog into an outgoing one. "Shy" dogs who have reformed were probably either undersocialized green dogs or yellow dogs who were able to "go green." Very shy dogs will stay true to their nature.

You can, however, improve the shy dog. The younger you start working with a shy dog, the more success you will have. But your socialization work will never be done. Even if you work hard for the first three years to expose a red dog to things he is uncertain of, he will still tend toward episodes of shyness—it's his nature. Shyness can create insecurity, and that insecurity will work to reinforce the dog's shyness.

How To Socialize a Shy Dog

When working with a shy dog, make sure that his experiences are positive and that he doesn't become overwhelmed. You'll need to learn to read your dog to determine if he is becoming overwhelmed. Many overwhelmed dogs will pull backward on the leash and not want to move forward. Some dogs will crouch as they walk. Dropped ears and a clamped tail are also signs, as is a hunched back. Some dogs will show worry in their eyes. If you let your dog become overwhelmed and don't resolve the problem, he will become less secure. If you see any of these signals from your dog, get him back to a place where he can regain a comfortable, relaxed feeling.

Socializing With Other Dogs

Some young dogs are so insecure that they become instantly overwhelmed in puppy class. In fact, the more outgoing dogs in the class may do more harm than good because they might frighten the more timid dogs. Start socializing your shy dog with just one dog—either a more timid puppy or a mature adult who is secure around a timid dog—and let your shy dog get used to him. Some dogs will need to stay at the one-on-one socializing stage for a long time before

An insecure young dog may become overwhelmed in puppy class.

159

A Lack of Self-Confidence

Dogs of any breed or pack status can suffer from poor self-confidence. Problems in dogs who lack self-confidence (or who rely too much on their owners for security) include excessive barking, attention seeking, fear-based aggression, health disorders, and sometimes self-mutilation. Dogs need to feel confident in themselves—but not so confident that they won't listen to their owners.

Here are some tips when dealing with a dog who lacks self-confidence.

- When walking your dog, do not keep him on a tight lead, especially when you meet other dogs. You will only encourage him to be afraid of the other dog. He may also feel trapped on a tight lead, which may cause him to feel that he must attack before he is attacked.
- Unless your dog is in immediate danger, don't pick him up when he becomes frightened. Dogs must learn to deal with their fears with all four paws on the ground.
- Don't let your dog become overwhelmed. If he is afraid of other dogs, don't plunge him into a situation in which he is going to become so frightened that he can't think but can only react. Learn to judge the limits of your dog—some dogs are frightened about things that other dogs will ignore.
- When working with your dog to overcome his fears about strange dogs, work him only around reliable dogs who won't harm or upset him.
- Keep your cool when your dog panics. Don't start jerking on the leash or yelling at the other dog. Use a confident and reassuring voice and a steady pace to help calm him down.

they feel confident enough to accept a few dogs at the same time. Some shyer puppies may be timid at first, then suddenly warm up to another dog. If this happens, consider yourself lucky! However, don't hesitate to run interference if your shy dog seems to become overwhelmed when playing with a strange dog.

Dog Introductions

One way to introduce your dog to a strange dog is to go for a walk with the dog you want to introduce. When dogs walk side by side in harmony, they often begin to feel comfortable with each other. The walk can also expel nervous energy an insecure dog may have built up. Be sure to walk with a dog who doesn't focus on your dog but on the walk. This will help your dog feel that he can ignore the newcomer. Once your dog has relaxed with another dog, let them greet each other. Let your dog greet the other dog first. Once your dog seems comfortable, allow the other dog to inspect your dog. Always keep both dogs under control by leashing them.

Introducing Your Dog to Strangers

A shy dog should be introduced to many different people before he begins to feel at ease with strangers. Walking your dog alongside a strange person before making an introduction can allow him to relax before meeting that new person. Once he seems to have settled down, you can let him meet with the person one-on-one.

Go for a walk with the dogs you want to introduce (below), and once they relax, they can get to know each other (right).

When Dogs Lunge at a Fence

Dogs who bark and lunge behind their fence can be upsetting to a more fearful or shyer dog who's walking on a leash. Even dogs who are not at all dog aggressive or fearful of other dogs can become dangerously out of control in this kind of situation. A dog can become so upset that he may escalate into dangerous behaviors. Whining and pulling back or surging forward on the leash is often the first hint that your dog is becoming upset. If you don't successfully reassure him and defuse his worries about these hostile fence lungers, he may progress to grabbing and biting at the leash. Dogs can become completely out of control and may bite or grab at their owners. Your dog may act aggressively toward the dog behind the fence in self-defense, and this once-amiable dog could turn into a dog-aggressive dog.

This is a problem that dog owners must resolve as soon as possible. There have been some who have tried to resolve this fear response in their dogs by putting a choke collar at the top of the neck and keeping strong tension to prevent them from reacting. This is a poor technique—the constant choking may keep a dog from reacting but does not solve his fear of the frightening dog behind the fence. With this kind of issue, seek professional help.

A great way to start the socialization process with a shy dog is to have one person at a time work with him. Find people your dog doesn't know who are willing to help and have some time to work with him.

Teach helpers the correct way to greet a shy dog:

1. Lower yourself to the dog's eye level.
2. Do not stare into the dog's eyes.
3. First, offer your hand for him to sniff.
4. Speak the dog's name in a low and calm tone.
5. If he is receptive and doesn't pull back on the leash, slowly move your hand toward his neck.
6. From the neck, you can trace your hand around the jaw and finally up to the head.

Do not try to plunge your hand toward a shyer dog's head—some dogs react poorly to that approach. If at any point your dog resists or moves away, let him. Never try to force him toward someone or block his escape—it can be dangerous.

Once your dog is relaxed around the new person, end the session for the day. This allows him time to think things over and realize that strangers are not bad. The next time you take your dog out to socialize him one-on-one with a stranger, you can introduce a second person if he seems to relax fairly quickly. After slowly building in quantity, you may find your dog becoming more comfortable around strangers.

Reach under the chin to pet a shyer dog.

The Treat Technique

One technique for socializing a shy dog with people is to hand out treats to strangers when you are out with him. Then bring your dog to those people one at a time and let him get a treat from them. This can greatly ease some dogs' uncertainty around strange people—after all, how bad can these people be when they hand out goodies?

There are a few guidelines to keep in mind with this technique. If your shy dog will not allow strangers to touch him, ask the people feeding the treats not to attempt to pet him but just to give a treat. Depending on your dog, you may need to work up to letting the stranger touch him when he doles out the treat.

When you feel that your dog is secure enough to allow a stranger to touch him while getting a treat, make sure that the stranger uses the correct technique. (See "Introducing Your Dog to Strangers.) Don't let someone reach down toward the top of your dog's head until you are sure that he will not react adversely to this action. Never force your dog to tolerate touch. Let him pull away from a touch if he wants to.

Desensitizing "Nervous Nellies"

A Little Play Can Break the Ice

When socializing your shy dog, try having a stranger throw his favorite ball. Even if your dog brings the ball back to you instead of the stranger, it may help him take a liking to the new person. You can always hand the ball back for the stranger to throw again.

Dogs Who Trick When There Are Treats

Some clever dogs learn how to eat the treat offered by a stranger but avoid being touched. By avoiding the human contact and getting the treat, these dogs will still require socialization. To correct this, consider enlisting the help of an experienced dog handler.

The dog handler will need a chewy dog biscuit, one that your dog can't quickly eat. Have the handler hold the treat in one hand and hold her free hand next to the treat. When your dog begins to eat the biscuit, the handler can slowly pull back the treat hand while leaving her free hand in place. For your dog to continue to chew the biscuit, he will be forced to brush against the handler's hand. Some dogs may pull away at first. Let your dog know that he can escape if he wants but that he can't continue to eat the treat when he pulls away. Simply reset the hands to the beginning position and start again. Typically, a dog will decide to finish the treat and not worry about being touched. After a time or two, most dogs will allow the

handler to pet them a little. This technique allows your dog to associate the touch with something positive, like eating a treat.

Handing Off Your Dog for Someone to Hold

With a shy dog who doesn't show any aggression (like biting), you can often socialize him by letting strangers hold him. Sometimes a dog will be more receptive if

You must let your dog relax when he is introduced to any new person.

Cookie Was Scared After Being Held

My Jack Russell Terrier, Cookie, was a shyer dog. Years ago, a trainer told me to let strangers hold her to help get her over her fears. I knew a man who'd worked with a lot of Jack Russell Terriers, so I gave him my dog to hold. He held Cookie for a few minutes, then gave her back. To my surprise, Cookie was even more afraid of strangers. I later discovered what had gone wrong. The entire time the man held my dog, Cookie remained tense. He did not hold her long enough to a point where she relaxed.

To correct this, I found a woman who was willing to take the time to help. The woman held Cookie for a very long time. She did not coddle my dog but merely held her in a friendly manner. After almost 20 minutes, Cookie relaxed and the woman returned my dog to me. After that one time, Cookie became more confident with strange people.

One of the biggest socialization mistakes you can make is to not let your dog relax during the time he is introduced to a new person, a new dog, or a stressful situation.

the stranger has just taken him on a short walk and he's had time to relax with the new person while on the leash.

To ensure that handing off your dog is successful, you must give him the opportunity to relax while someone holds him. Depending on how insecure he is or what socialization stage he's at, this can take from a few minutes to half an hour. Make sure that you and the person have the time to commit to this exercise before you try.

Highly Sensitive Dogs

The degree of sensitivity in dogs can vary. The highly sensitive dog reacts more acutely to the behaviors of people that other dogs may ignore or not find distressing. A highly sensitive dog may also overreact to reprimands, a harsh tone of voice, and mood changes in people. These dogs may become quite upset when their owners are angry. Some tune in to an owner's illness, while others may react adversely when their owners are nervous. It isn't unusual for a highly sensitive dog to become very stressed over what he senses, which could cause him to bite.

Highly Sensitive Dogs and Corrections

Highly sensitive dogs can become quite distressed when reprimanded or corrected.

165

Lestat the Brat Was Sensitive

Sometimes certain dog traits make an animal frustrating to train. Lestat was not only very determined to do things his way, but he was equally as sensitive to any corrections. On an agility course, he'd often decide on his own what obstacles to take (over my directions). However, when I'd tell him "No," his tail would drop, his head would lower, and he'd call it quits—sometimes he'd even leave the course. It was Lestat who forced me to learn how to keep things positive when working for compliance.

Lestat was also extremely sensitive in other areas. Once, when I had the 24-hour flu, he surprised me. I'd spent the day throwing up, and when I went to bed that night, he jumped onto the corner of my bed. He had never jumped on my bed before (or since), but he knew that something was very wrong with me, and jumping onto my bed to stay nearby was the only assistance he could offer.

That's what can make these kinds of dogs so difficult. I hate how overly sensitive he is to any corrections—especially because he is so strong willed about doing things his way. But his oversensitivity when trying to make sure that I'm taken care of is so touching.

It isn't unusual for these dogs to become so focused on the correction that they will completely miss why they were corrected. What a dog might find too harsh will vary—for some dogs, a tug on the leash can be too traumatic; for others, a harsh tone of voice may be shattering.

When dealing with a dog who has an acutely sensitive nature, the owner must learn how to correct misbehaviors in a way that won't cause the animal to overreact. Deciding on the right correction will depend on the dog. Some dogs who don't have enough confidence in their owners will not tolerate any correction—even a verbal "no."

With this kind of dog, you will need to work your training from a "reward the desired behavior" perspective only. As your dog grows more confident with your training, you can begin to use an "et" sound to show disapproval. If you feel that your dog is not cooperating at all, try a time-out in a crate to help him focus on what you want.

Positive, reward-based training is essential. When you are training, lure your dog into the desired behavior, and never force him. While this is true for any dog, it's especially true for the highly sensitive dog—it is better to train for what you want instead of disciplining what you don't want.

Highly Reactive Dogs

A highly reactive dog responds acutely to stimuli to which most other dogs are indifferent. Some are very noise sensitive. Others may jump away from slight movements that are not even threatening. Because of their highly reactive nature, you'll need to spend time desensitizing these dogs.

Why are some dogs highly reactive? Surely people wouldn't breed a dog to be that way? I suspect that we have done that very thing. There are advantages to high reactivity in some circumstances, such as reacting to slight movements and noises to stay safe. For example, a herding dog must detect and react to a slight movement from an animal to control it. The almost too-quick-for-thought reaction can also help a dog escape a flying hoof to the head—a dog who doesn't act quickly could get seriously hurt. High reactivity provides the skills needed by some dogs in certain professions. Unfortunately, many dog owners find these skills a problem and must learn to correctly train them.

Desensitization Guidelines

Dogs who are highly reactive require a lot of desensitization to inert things in their surroundings. When working with this kind of dog, you must:

- do the training in the right order
- use distance to your advantage
- be sure that your dog reaches a calm state while training
- never force your dog

A herding dog needs to detect and react to slight movements to do his job—this can make for a highly reactive dog.

The Order for Desensitization

The correct order to desensitize a dog is to first introduce him to the noise or other distressful issue, then introduce the reward. This allows him to associate the noise with something positive.

Using the wrong order when working to desensitize a dog can actually *create* anxiety. I use the example of Sydney, a Labrador Retriever, as a cautionary tale. Sydney's owner, Harold, wanted to desensitize him to the sound of a rifle being discharged. Harold knew that the noise from his hunting rifle could be upsetting to a dog, so he got proactive about training him. Because Sydney loved to play ball, Harold decided that the best way to work with him was to get him to associate the sound of the rifle with something good, like playing with a ball—a great technique for desensitization.

Harold spent several days in a row throwing the ball for Sydney, then shooting off a shotgun—*the wrong order for desensitization*! By throwing the ball first, Sydney associated that action with something bad to follow, which was the blast of the shotgun. Sydney got to the point where he would shake any time a ball was picked up. Not only did he not learn to become comfortable with the noise of a shotgun, but he refused to ever play ball again.

When desensitizing your dog, make sure he's not so overwhelmed that he won't accept a treat.

168

Distance Can Help Desensitize

When working to desensitize your dog, make sure that he's not so overwhelmed that he's too upset to accept a treat or a play reward. When this happens, you must take him farther away from the stimulus that is upsetting him. Find a distance where he has a very mild reaction to the event, and begin working to calm your dog at that location. You can then begin to bring him closer and closer to whatever is upsetting him, and slowly work toward getting him to settle down long enough to focus on the reward.

Your Dog Must Feel at Ease

Your dog must feel at ease during the desensitization process. Too often, the entire time an owner is attempting to calm his dog, he never settles down. Even if the dog accepts food, he still may be stressed. Dogs who are stressed may pull on the leash as if in a hurry, tuck in their tails, pucker the skin above the eyes, or whine. If your dog never relaxes during the time you are introducing something stressful, you haven't succeeded. Use a calming tone of voice while you are giving treats to or petting your dog. Once he calms down, offer a jackpot of treats and praise. Learn how to communicate with a "Hey buddy, we did it!" tone that tells your dog you approve of this new behavior.

Don't Try to Force a Dog

Trying to force a dog into a situation where he is very uncomfortable is not a good way to train him to relax. Let your dog choose to accept what is stressing him out instead of forcing him to do so. For example, when starting out in agility, some dogs fear the dogwalk obstacle. I've seen some trainers place their dogs on the top of the obstacle and hold them there. But a better way, especially with a sensitive dog,

Try looking over your shoulder at a sensitive dog—he may consider this less threatening.

would be to introduce him a little at a time to the obstacle. Put your dog about 1 foot (.3 m) from the end of the exit ramp of the dogwalk, and allow him to walk off those few steps under his own power. If he seems comfortable with that, set him 2 feet (.6 m) from the end of the dogwalk. Now work backward 1 foot (.3 m) at a time. Don't continue to ask for more and more from your dog if he's uncertain. Be sure to make your last effort a successful one, even if you have to repeat a previous level and end after that success.

Training Challenges of Combination Dogs

Dealing with a highly sensitive dog takes a lot of work, as does dealing with a highly reactive dog, and it isn't unusual to find both in the same package. Add a shyer nature and you have a real training challenge on your hands. Although any mixture of these traits can be combined in some dogs, many of the training techniques to resolve these issues overlap and can be combined to create a more stable dog.

Playing

Play is often a great tool to help a challenging dog overcome his fears. I've seen many shyer dogs, who don't consider a treat enough incentive to find a stranger comforting, warm up with play. Some dogs who feel stressed in a strange environment will forget about their worries if their owners take out a familiar toy for some intense play. Play also helps a dog associate a perceived fearful situation with a good experience.

Dog's Who Won't Play

Some dogs actually need to be taught how to play with their owners. Because there is a great bonding benefit to play, it's a worthwhile venture. If your dog won't play, you might want to try letting him see another dog playing. Some dogs will pick up on the activity if they see another dog doing it. Letting your dog watch another dog run after a ball can build some excitement for him to do the same. Also, use a happy, excited voice when offering a toy. Try lots of different toys to find one your dog

likes—squeaky, fur covered, bouncy, rubber, cloth—there's a huge variety available. When first working to get your dog to play with you, keep the lessons short.

Calming Signals

Kelly Misegadis, owner of a champion Boston Terrier, first introduced me to calming techniques. Calming signals are based on Turid Rugaas' influential and well-respected book, *On Talking Terms With Dogs: Calming Signals*, which is an extremely helpful reference for dealing with any dog. Kelly showed me a very practical way to apply the information in the book.

Kelly used Turid's calming techniques

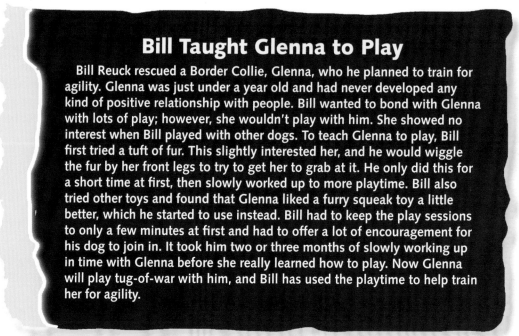

Bill Taught Glenna to Play

Bill Reuck rescued a Border Collie, Glenna, who he planned to train for agility. Glenna was just under a year old and had never developed any kind of positive relationship with people. Bill wanted to bond with Glenna with lots of play; however, she wouldn't play with him. She showed no interest when Bill played with other dogs. To teach Glenna to play, Bill first tried a tuft of fur. This slightly interested her, and he would wiggle the fur by her front legs to try to get her to grab at it. He only did this for a short time at first, then slowly worked up to more playtime. Bill also tried other toys and found that Glenna liked a furry squeak toy a little better, which he started to use instead. Bill had to keep the play sessions to only a few minutes at first and had to offer a lot of encouragement for his dog to join in. It took him two or three months of slowly working up in time with Glenna before she really learned how to play. Now Glenna will play tug-of-war with him, and Bill has used the playtime to help train her for agility.

to help get her Boston out of respiratory distress and found that the techniques helped calm many dogs struggling with nervousness and unease. Start by stroking your dog under his neck to calm him, or you can use a less hands-on technique, such as the visual cue of yawning. Because Kelly had already trained her dog to pay attention when she used his name, she'd wait until Hoosier made eye contact with her. Then she'd give the verbal command "Get it together," immediately followed by deep, slow yawns.

Kelly recommends that you polish your yawns. Before you yawn, drop your shoulders, which provides another relaxing visual cue to your dog. Another cue is to slow your breathing and relax mentally. Try tipping your head sideways, and avoid making eye contact, then give a wide-mouthed yawn. If your dog is too keyed up to relax after a couple yawns, ask him to settle again, then turn your back on him. You can peek out of the corner of your eyes to check on his reaction.

Try using calming signals in a less stressful area. Oftentimes a dog is more relaxed at home, so that's a great place to start. Once you get the basics down, you can then work at the place where your dog often becomes stressed. For example, if he becomes stressed at shows, take him to one when he's not entered so that you can focus on training. Mimic all the things you normally do when showing. Don't be surprised if your dog begins to get a little anxious from the moment you take him out of the crate. If he's so nervous by the time

Like petting, massage can soothe some dogs.

you get ringside that he can't focus on your calming signals, move your lesson away from the area that causes anxiousness. Find a quiet corner at the dog show and work there. Once you have success, you can work up to the area where he has difficulty.

Calming signals can be self-perpetuating. People often hunch their shoulders when they are uptight, and their breathing becomes more shallow and rapid. However, when you drop your shoulders, quiet your breathing, and use a wide-mouthed yawn, you will find your own nervousness coming under control. This quieter demeanor will be picked up by your dog and create a calming all its own. Many people don't realize that they are giving cues to their dog that create stress. Make a checklist as you are working with your dog: body posture, muscle tension, and tone of voice. You must relax for your sensitive dog to feel at ease.

Massage

Like petting, massage can soothe some dogs. Massaging releases endorphins, which helps a dog relax. Do a little research before you begin. There are books and DVDs available that can show you how to properly massage your dog.

To get started, lay him on his side, talk calmly, and stroke him to help him relax. Then gently and slowly rock his body back and forth. This warm-up targets the mobility of the joints.

Rub the muscles in a circular motion using light compression. Make sure that you don't rub down to the bone. A massage

Kelly is giving her dog a calming signal—a yawn.

should feel good to your dog, so don't rub too hard or you could bruise the tissue. Be careful because the more stoic breeds will not let you know when a rub is too hard. You may want to use a word like "easy" or "relax" while you massage so that later you can cue your dog to settle down when he is in a stressful situation using the same word.

Do not force your dog to accept a massage. If he seems resistant, make sure that you aren't being too rough. If he seems uninterested, you may want to experiment with rubbing a different area.

Building Confidence

With insecure dogs, a little confidence building can be very valuable. Some problems with dogs stem from a lack of self-confidence or reliance on their owners holding them for security. This can cause problems like excessive barking, attention seeking, and sometimes self-mutilation. Dogs need to feel confident in themselves but not so confident that they become unmanageable. My thanks to trainer Kim Gillespie, who shared her insights regarding this issue. She learned a lot about building confidence in dogs, especially after she rescued two Italian Greyhounds.

Patience

Working to build confidence takes time, so patience is key. Oftentimes, you will need to do a lot of desensitization while working to build your dog's confidence. With encouragement, he will learn to relax if he isn't pushed or rushed and if you keep the situation secure and upbeat. You can't force, scold, or bully your dog into a comfort zone, so never punish him for being stressed out.

What works is to push a little, then get your dog to relax in the new situation. If he becomes progressively less comfortable or can't settle back down, then it is time to stop the training session. Depending on your

Praise

Be quick to praise behaviors you want in your dog, and try not to criticize the ones you don't.

dog's stress level, the session might begin again in a few minutes, or you may have to give him more time off. When the session resumes, never hesitate to backtrack a step or two to help him regain his confidence.

Find the Right Place

To build confidence, your dog must be exposed to a variety of people, other dogs, and situations. Find places where he will have success, and avoid loose dogs, unmanaged children, and large crowds until he has had a chance to build up his confidence.

Don't Coddle

Often, owners are too quick to coddle their dogs when they overreact to things that upset them, especially if the dogs are easy to pick up and will readily curl up in their arms. Coddling is a bad thing for a dog's confidence. Picking up a dog for every little issue will create an insecure animal. Unless your dog is in danger, give him the opportunity to stand up to his own fears at ground level.

Meeting Other Dogs

When out for a walk, do not keep your dog on a tight lead—especially when you

Desensitizing "Nervous Nellies"

173

Don't Panic

Sensitive dogs tend to be quite aware of their owners' moods. Keep your cool when out with your dog so that he doesn't panic when a strange dog approaches.

meet other dogs. You will only encourage him to be afraid of the other dogs. Your dog may also feel trapped on a tight lead, which could lead to him feeling like he must attack before he is attacked. If you have access to a self-assured dog, one with whom your dog feels comfortable, take that dog along with you. The self-assured dog can teach yours how to settle down and even how to greet other people and other dogs.

Your attitude is just as important. When greeting a strange dog, keep a confident attitude. Remember that a dog, especially one who's more sensitive, will pick up behavior patterns from his surroundings. If you are nervous and stressed, your dog will pick up that stress from you.

Loud Noises

Some very sensitive dogs can quickly become unraveled upon hearing loud noises. Find a quiet place to do any introductions. If your dog starts to get upset after hearing a loud noise, don't raise your voice because it will only increase his stress. Instead, use a calm and reassuring tone of voice. If the noise repeats, toss a

treat after it sounds, as if the unnerving noise was a cue for a treat. This will help your dog redefine the unpleasant situation as one that is more pleasant.

Games

You can use play to build confidence. Dogs who need confidence can benefit from a game of tug-of-war (but don't try it if your dog has aggression issues). Also, try a "chase me to get a toy" game, which offers fun interaction, and you can praise your dog for "winning." The "winning" process does wonders for a dog's confidence. End all play sessions on a positive note, with your dog wanting more.

Clicker

While I don't go into clicker training in this book, it can work well to shape desired behaviors and inch a dog toward things of which he is less sure. Eventually, he can learn that those things are not a threat, which

Desensitization to Noises

Kim Gillespie found out that one of her Italian Greyhounds, Boomer, had a problem with noise after she decided to buy a soda. The sound of the can rattling out of the machine freaked Boomer out, so Kim spent some time desensitizing him right there on the spot. She showed Boomer the soda can. Then she brought him up to the machine and let him see that it wasn't going to bite him. She put the soda can back in the dispensing slot and rattled it around a bit, then took it out again and showed it to him. After a few times, Boomer realized that there was nothing to worry about.

Kim also had to get Boomer used to the sound of her treadmill. She starting by turning the treadmill on low, then grabbing some dog treats. Kim held Boomer on a leash at a distance far enough away that he was not stressed about the noise. By feeding him treats while the treadmill was running, Boomer learned to associate the noise with something good. As her dog became more and more comfortable with the noise, Kim moved him closer and closer until he was so confident that he was willing to step onto the treadmill while it was running.

These Italian Greyhounds have a tendency toward shyness and reactivity.

in turn can enable him to release that particular fear. There are many books available that explain in detail how to clicker train a dog.

Ultimately, no matter what type of training you use, if you teach your dog what behaviors are acceptable and what's expected of him—in the home environment as well as when engaging with the outside world—he'll be a much more confident dog and in turn will be more relaxed and happier overall.

Stop Before You Get Frustrated

Stop training when your dog gets stubborn rather than let yourself become frustrated. Frustration will come across too negatively to a sensitive dog. Learn to do something different that is positive so that your dog doesn't pick up on your frustration. Also, watch for when your dog loses interest in the task. If he loses interest, move on to something else.

ProblemBehaviors and CaseStudies

PartFour

Chapter Ten

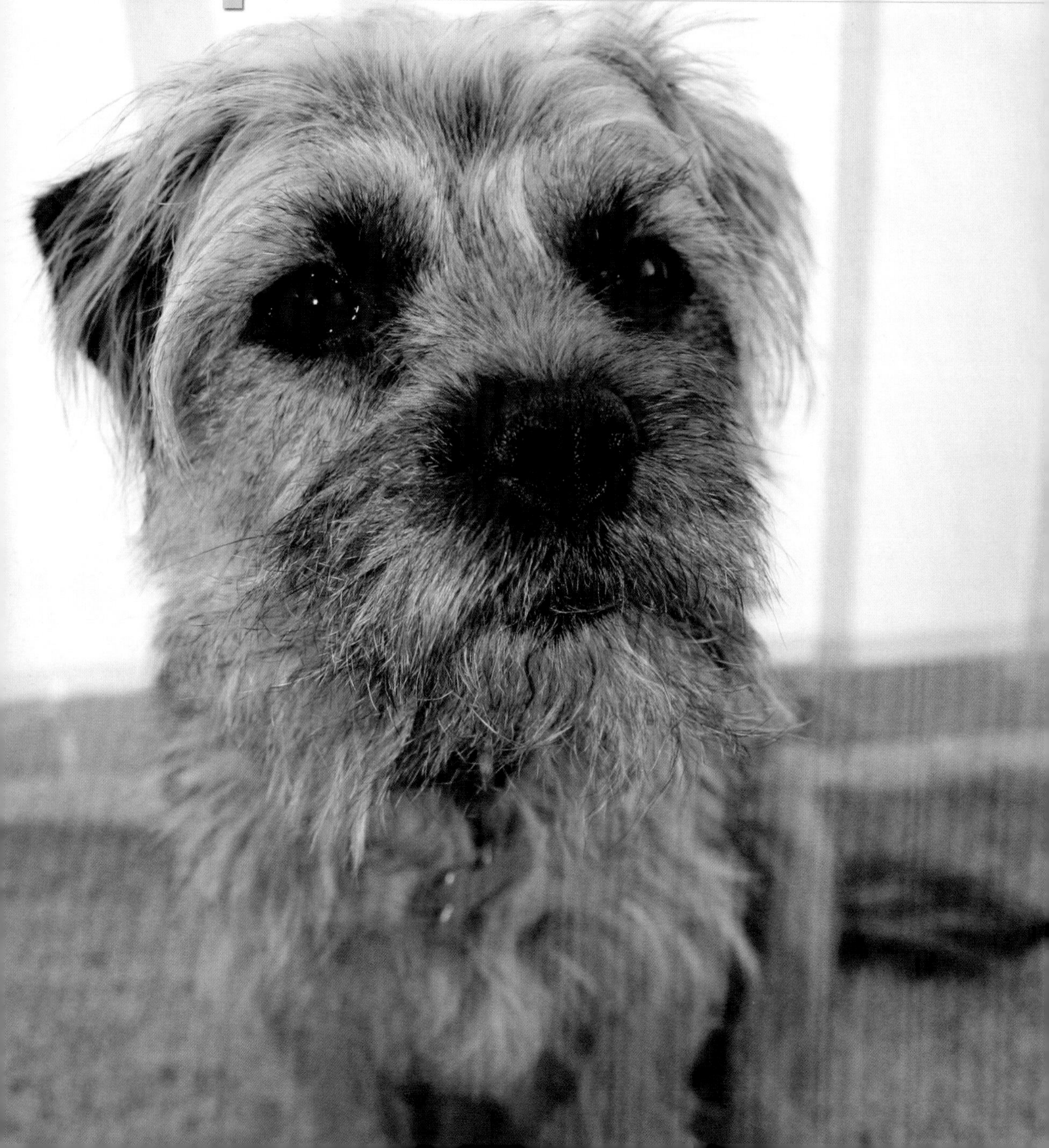

Housetraining and Marking Issues

People have been housetraining dogs for generations, yet many problems surround this training. Sometimes, problems arise because the housetraining process was not done correctly. After all, the old-fashioned idea of rubbing a dog's nose into mistakes still persists, even though more modern and effective ideas—like rewarding a dog for eliminating in the correct spot—exist. Sometimes the type of breed is a factor or whether the dog has been neutered or spayed.

After explaining how to housetrain, we'll move on to the seemingly unsolvable housetraining issues that can arise with some dogs, and we'll also discuss marking issues.

Housetraining a Dog

If you are having housetraining issues, ask yourself if you understand all the factors that affect housetraining, such as age, and have reasonable expectations of your dog. Then, go back and make sure that you've housetrained your dog correctly and consistently using the method described below.

Dogs less than a year old can have poor bladder control.

Age and Control

With most dogs, bladder control takes much longer to master than bowel control. The age at which a dog has the physical ability to control the urge to urinate can be as early as a few months old to seven or eight months old. Sometimes younger dogs will seem to achieve bladder control, only to falter when playing. As dogs reach their senior years, bladder control can again wane.

Reasonable Expectations

Sometimes the problem with housetraining is that the owner doesn't understand what to expect. Just the other day I heard someone complain about a ten-week-old puppy who seemed to be housetrained but had regressed. The owner did not understand what he could expect with a young dog. Here are some reasonable expectations with regard to bladder control:

- Most larger breeds may have sufficient bowel and bladder control to be somewhat reliably trained by three months.
- Most smaller breeds will not have control until they are several months old, and some won't have it until they are almost a year old.
- Even a three- to four-month-old dog who can hold his urine for up to hours at a time may not have much control when he plays. The physical ability to hold urine while playing can take a lot longer to gain than the ability to hold urine when the dog is less active.

Poor Bladder Control in Younger Dogs

Dogs under a year of age can have poor bladder control. Although a dog may let you know when it is time to go outside, occasionally when playing, he'll suddenly stop and squat to expel a small amount of urine. Although this is frustrating, never yell at your dog when he pees in the house. Yelling or punishing him for accidents will only encourage him to hide this problem and won't teach him what you actually want him to do—ask to go outside. As your dog matures, he will be better able to hold urine for longer periods and will learn to control the urge when playing. While waiting for your dog to outgrow this issue, clean away the smells from any accidents using and enzymatic cleaner and encourage him to make it outside to urinate.

Schedule

Getting your dog on a schedule is one of the first steps to successful housetraining. Feed him on a rigid schedule, then watch carefully for the typical time at which things come out the other end. By figuring out your dog's normal elimination schedule, you can make sure that he's in an area in which you want him to eliminate. Typically, the younger the dog, the quicker he'll eliminate after eating. As your dog grows, he'll be able to wait longer after he eats a meal before he needs to eliminate.

Confinement

Once you have your dog on a schedule, make sure that you are around to take him out. Puppies used to be paper trained, but this technique has fallen out of vogue. Many people find that the best solution is to teach a dog to go outside from the beginning.

When you first begin to housetrain, use a crate to confine your dog when you are gone. However, if you must leave your young dog home for more hours than he can hold it, you'll need to make other arrangements. Perhaps he could be let out by a neighbor or a friend, or you could have a doggy door installed so that he can go outside when he needs to. If none of these options is available, restrict your dog to a pen where he can sleep in one area and eliminate in another area covered in paper.

Crates are a great way to housetrain a dog. Dogs, by nature, want to keep their sleeping area clean. Confining a dog in a crate encourages him to hold his urine and feces because he won't want to soil his sleeping area. And because a dog is less active when in a crate, he'll need to go less often. If you choose to restrict your younger dog to a pen because you are gone for

Activity

The more active a dog is, the more frequently he will need to eliminate. This is why a puppy may sleep through the night without needing to go outside but fail to make it more than a few hours during the day.

longer than he can hold it, when he gets old enough to hold it during the day, he can be switched to a crate only.

Once you get home, your first task should be to escort him outside to where you want

him to go. Use the treat and leash method described in the next section. If your dog does have an accident when you confine him to the crate, thoroughly clean up the bedding. Don't panic if he has a few accidents that first week. However, if after two weeks your dog is still not keeping his crate clean, go back to the arrangement mentioned earlier, where the dog is in a restricted area and can exit the crate on his own to eliminate. One way to help secure success is to take a walk in the morning to encourage your dog to eliminate before crate confinement. Although it's not always

Use a crate to confine your dog when you are gone.

Never Over-Crate a Dog

Many dogs find crates reassuring, but too much time in a crate is not good. A dog who shows anxiety while inside the enclosure may be reacting to too much crate time. Some will even take up excessive licking and create raw areas on their legs. Use the crate wisely; a rule of thumb is that puppies can hold it for one hour per month of age, which means that a dog less than six months of age cannot be expected to control his bladder for more than a few hours at a time. If you have to be away from home more than four or five hours a day, you must make arrangements for him to either be let out or to be confined in an area where he can answer the call without eliminating in the crate.

convenient, by dedicating a week or so in the initial housetraining stage, you can help secure success.

Going Outside

Don't just put your dog outside (in a fenced-in area, of course) and hope that he does his business. Escorting him outside is a much better method. Even if you have a fenced yard, put your dog on a leash and go for a walk around the backyard. Reward him when he eliminates where you want him to. Praise him and offer a treat after he has finished his business. It is my personal philosophy to use a special treat, one that a dog likes more than normal. I want him to quickly become invested in doing his business where I want him to rather than in a place he finds more convenient.

Not only will accompanying your dog outside allow you to reward him, but you will be better able to make sure that he has actually eliminated before coming back into the house. Not escorting your dog outside can be the cause of intermittent success. If you're not there, you will never know that he only peed, and you'll be left wondering why he came back in and had an accident on the rug. In the early stage of housetraining, putting in time and effort to get things started correctly can set the stage for later success.

Encourage Bladder Control

There is a technique that helps some dogs with poor bladder control learn how to go outside for those small, hard-to-control potty breaks. Instead of yelling when he starts to eliminate inside, train your dog using a verbal command like "Outside." When you see him squat, say "Outside" in a pleasant and slightly enthusiastic tone, then shove a tasty and great-smelling treat under his nose and lead him outside with that treat. Don't expect your dog to abandon peeing immediately the first time you do this, but work to divert him from answering the call.

With this training technique, you are hoping for two things. First, you are trying to train your dog to run for the door sooner when those urges occur. Second, by encouraging your young dog to interrupt the urine flow and pursue the treat, you can help him begin to build bladder control sooner. Don't expect him to be immediately reformed with this technique. However, with persistence, your dog can learn to stop peeing and to dash for the door during this difficult developmental period.

Dealing With Accidents

Don't punish your dog for having an accident inside the house. Scolding a dog or pushing his nose in the mess can teach him to get sneaky about doing his business in the house, when what you really want is to train him to go outside. Making matters worse, punishment for elimination will work against outdoor training because you

Don't just put your dog outside and hope that he does his business—put him on a leash and escort him outside.

Praise your dog when he goes outside.

are unintentionally training your dog not to eliminate in your presence.

If your dog has an accident in the house or soils the inside of the crate, clean up the area as soon as possible. The odor must be removed, not simply masked, or he may decide to eliminate in that area again. There are many products on the market that use enzymes to clear away the unwanted material and ensure that the odor is removed. Check with your local pet supplier to find these products.

If you suspect that your dog has had accidents inside the house but don't know if you have found all the areas to neutralize the odor, specialized ultraviolet lights can help you find urine on the carpet and walls.

Housetraining Problems

Sometimes, even if you have taken the time to correctly housetrain your dog, problems will occur. First, take him to the vet and have him examined. Some problems are due to medical issues. If he's been given the all clear from your vet, you must figure out what the issue is and take time to correct it.

If Your Dog Chronically Eliminates in the House

"I give up! My dog Darma won't stop messing in the house. I let her out every half an hour, but that doesn't help. She just won't stop going wherever she pleases."

With a mature dog who chronically eliminates in the house, controlling his environment will help the most. Here are

Don't yell at or scold your dog when accidents happen.

some things you can do for this problem:

- Confine your dog when you cannot watch him, either in his crate or in a penned-off area inside the house.
- When you are home, don't let your dog have free run of the house. Put his leash on and hold onto it, or tie it to yourself. Don't let him out of your sight.
- If your dog has an accident when tethered to you, take him and the mess outside and use the command "Outside."
- Feed your dog on a strict schedule.

- When you get home, take him outside for exercise. Schedule time for at least a one-hour walk.
- If your dog answers the call of nature, be ready with a reward and praise.
- If he doesn't answer the call, up his activity level with running or high-energy playing to stimulate his system.
- You might want to give clicker training a try. Click and treat your dog several times to get him used to the idea that a click means a reward. Then take the clicker with you outside. Click and treat any squatting motion to help shape the

behavior you want.

- At night, schedule another walk before bedtime.
- Do not yell at your dog or scold him at any time. Train from a reward-only perspective.

Although this can be a tedious process, your dog will typically become more reliable after a few weeks. When you decide to give him more freedom, keep him on a feeding schedule and continue to escort him outside so that you can reward the correct behavior. Also, be diligent about watching for accidents, and clean them up thoroughly if you find them. When accidents happen, don't hesitate to again confine your dog for a while afterward, but do give him another chance at freedom in the house. If accidents keep happening, you may want to tether him to you for a while. Some dogs seem to feel that it's okay to sneak off when their owners aren't looking to do their business. By tethering your dog, you can make sure that he learns to go outside when he needs to answer the call. Retraining your dog can take time, but once he realizes the reward of going outside, he'll soon become committed to doing his business there.

If Your Dog Chronically Eliminates in the Crate

"My dog is two years old now, and I've tried everything and can't train her. She goes potty in her crate (which is small enough that she has to lie in it when she does). I have to clean poop and pee every day and then give her a bath. I am desperate for help."

Small Crates

Although there are lots of warnings about getting a crate that is too large, a crate that is too small can create housetraining issues. Make sure that your dog's crate is large enough so that if he does have an accident, he isn't forced to lie in his own mess.

A lot of information warns owners not to choose too large of a crate for a dog when first crate training. However, little information exists about the consequences of too small a crate. Young dogs can and often do have accidents inside the crate. Sometimes older dogs who have eaten something that didn't sit well may make a mess uncontrollably. Although you don't want a crate so large that your dog can use one end for a bathroom, you also don't want to use a crate so small that he is forced to lie in his waste. This disrupts his natural instinct to not eliminate in his sleeping area. Once your dog is chronically eliminating in his crate, you'll have some tedious retraining to do, but it can be done.

- Remove the too-small crate and confine your dog in a very large wire crate or an exercise pen.
- Put a pillow for sleeping in one end of the area.
- In the other end, make an area for elimination. Use dog litter, newspapers, puppy pads, or even dirt from outdoors.

- Scent the elimination area with a sample of poop and pee from your dog.
- Keep him inside this area when he is not with you in the house.
- It usually helps to get three or four pillows or towels to use as bedding. This way, you can more easily exchange the bedding as soon as your dog eliminates in the sleeping area.

Retraining a dog's natural instinct when he has learned to lie in his own waste takes a long time and a lot of cleaning. Be tenacious and patient. Typically, after a week, he may begin to keep his bedding clean. Expect more and more success as time goes by, but keep in mind that it isn't unusual for the process to take months—and you may see some regression. The better you are at keeping the sleeping area clean, the sooner you will have success.

Housetraining Regression

You may have a dog who seems reliably housetrained until one day he suddenly begins eliminating in the house. This is housetraining regression and may be age related or caused by a change in the household.

Age-Related Regression

"I came home the other day, and my seven-month-old Doberman Pinscher had trashed the place," one of my clients told me. "He was tearing up a pillow when I opened the door. There were poop piles on the floor. It looked like the dog had a private party. Now, the past few days, he doesn't

Sometimes spaying or neutering can help with age-related housetraining regression.

seem to bother to let me know when he needs to go out. Last night, I walked up and he looked right at me and peed."

My first thought was separation anxiety, a serious problem that can result in destructive behavior, typically right after the owner leaves. However, this adolescent dog seemed to trash the place at a later time and no longer acted housetrained, even when his owner was home—a telltale sign of housetraining regression. Call it an adolescent problem, but some dogs seem to forget that they were ever housetrained, starting as early as four months to almost a year old. This age-related issue can disappear on its own, or you many need to help resolve it. If you don't, your dog may carry the problem into adulthood.

Keeping a male or female intact increases the chances of age-related housetraining regression. With age-related regression, both males and females seem to forget their housetraining and may start to mark inside the house and may also leave poop piles. With females, the problem often escalates before she goes through her first heat cycle. Getting a dog spayed or neutered will help; however, once the dog gets into the habit of marking, it often needs to be addressed as a separate issue. (See "Marking.")

The Doberman who experienced age-related housetraining regression greatly benefited from being neutered, then going to obedience classes. Like many problems, the housetraining was only part of the issue. He was also out of control with his general behavior as well as housetraining, and his owners needed work with both to help re-establish control. The obedience classes helped, as did constructive exercise to help curb his destructive behavior.

Stress Can Lead to Regression

If your dog doesn't adapt well to changes, he may regress at any age. Introducing a

Adolescence and Regression

Housetraining regression frequently occurs around adolescence, between the ages of six months and one year. Spaying or neutering in a timely fashion increases the odds that you will escape this issue.

new dog into a household, moving, or a new baby doesn't sit well with all dogs and may cause stress in your pet. Sensitive dogs may regress with housetraining when the humans in the household become stressed.

The best way to solve housetraining regression is to retrain your dog as if he has never been housetrained. (At least now you have the advantage of an adult dog who can hold it for longer periods than a puppy!) Use a crate to confine him when you're not home, and crate him at home when you see regression issues. When you take your dog out of the crate, immediately take him outside on a leash. Even if you have to walk in circles in the backyard for a long time, stay with him until he's eliminated in the proper spot, and be prepared to offer a reward. Depending on your dog, you may only need to do this for a few days, or it may take a few weeks. By remaining patient in the early stages, you can facilitate the entire process.

When used properly, many dogs find crate time to be stabilizing. If you keep your dog in a crate while at home, move the crate with you from room to room. Crate him

189

with a positive attitude, and don't hesitate to treat in the crate. When working to resolve housetraining regression, dogs need reassurance, not discipline.

New Dogs Can Regress

Sometimes a newly adopted adult dog will regress with housetraining. When a mature dog is introduced into an established household, it may take a little time for him to adapt to the change and to your routine.

New dogs should be treated like a dog you are housetraining for the first time until they've had a chance to settle in. Some dogs are nervous when they first arrive in a new household and may need to eliminate more often. Other dogs may take a little while to get used to a new schedule. Don't punish accidents in the house; merely clean them up and continue with the housetraining schedule. Give your dog a week to settle in. If he still has issues after a week, use a crate for confinement, then take him outside on a leash, walk him until he eliminates, and reward him for going outside.

When introducing a new dog or a significant change to your household, crates can be a big help. A crate can be used to help establish control over bathroom times. Typically, a housetrained dog will work hard to keep the crate clean, so it helps make sure that he does his business outside. The crate will also allow him to have a safe haven in case you have other dogs in the house who need to adjust to the change. Insecure dogs may need a little more attention to reassure them during the adjustment period.

When Breed Is a Factor in Housetraining

Some breeds are notably more difficult to housetrain, including toy breeds such as the Affenpinscher and the Maltese. Some hounds, like the Beagle, and some terriers, like the Jack Russell Terrier, are also cited as more problematic.

Smaller dogs with thin coats can be harder to housetrain because they don't tolerate the cold well. Italian Greyhounds are a good example—not only are their coats thin, but these are sensitive dogs who will react adversely to negative training.

A newly adopted adult dog may regress with housetraining.

A Challenge With an Iggy

I know a rescued Italian Greyhound named Boomer who had never been reliably housetrained. Unfortunately, his previous owners had punished him for accidents, which made this very sensitive dog all the more of a challenge. Because he knew that he'd be punished for eliminating, he didn't want to do his business when people were watching. This made trying to take him outside and offering him a reward for correct behavior a challenge.

Boomer's owner, Kim Gillespie, used a clicker to help train him. After introducing her dog to the idea that a click meant a treat, Kim spent hours outside with him. Any time Boomer made any slight squatting movement, she clicked. This helped shape the behavior Kim wanted, and eventually her dog got over his intimidation about eliminating around people, which accelerated his housetraining enormously.

Reverse Housetraining

If your dog has a fine coat or is older and doesn't fare well in cold weather, one solution is to train your dog to use a litter box inside the house. Dog litter boxes can be purchased or made. Typically, the litter box higher sides so that the dog doesn't have issues with waste falling over the side. Try setting up an inside pen for your dog with a sleeping area and a litter box area. Daub some pee onto a paper towel and deposit it in the litter box; a poop sample can also be deposited. This will encourage your dog to use the inside litter box. You can also put the litter box outside for your dog to use. Once he gets the idea, move the box inside. Or if you have a garage, put the litter box there. When your dog understands how to use it, he can have free reign of the house again. Move any accidents into the litter box, and clean up the mess thoroughly.

Marking

Marking is when a dog urinates, usually small amounts, to leave his or her scent. Marking isn't about housetraining. Dogs who know how to go outside to do their business may still choose to mark in the house. Both males and females will mark, although the problem is more common with males. Intact dogs or dogs who were spayed or neutered at a late age have a higher likelihood of marking behavior. Often, an intact male who has been reliable in a household for years will mark when around a female in heat. Some breeds, such as

Dachshunds, just seem to have more of a tendency to mark.

Territory Marking

Territory marking typically begins during adolescence. Although a dog of higher pack status may be protecting territory, insecure dogs will also mark territory. Some dogs will go so far as to mark their owners' possessions.

The best way to curb territory marking is to be on the lookout for the problem. Sometimes a dog who never marked will begin to do so when a new dog is introduced or a household change occurs. Keep a watch out for any of these types of activities.

With some dogs, spaying or neutering will help even after the dog begins to mark territory. The quicker you alter a dog after you see the first signs of marking, the better your chances of stopping the issue. However, with a dog who has been intact for a while, two factors are working against you. First, the dog has formed a habit, and habits take time to break. Second, with many mature dogs who are neutered, it can take up to a year for the hormonal levels to subside, leaving their behavior slow to change.

If your dog begins marking, you must clean it up quickly and remove all traces of the smell— some dogs will persist if there is any trace of urine smell. The odor can even create problems when other dogs visit. I've seen females squat and leave a little tinkle because the homeowner didn't realize that there was a slight marking scent in that spot.

Get a belly band for males or britches for females who are marking. A belly band is a strip of material that is worn like a girdle around a male dog's belly. A pad is used to capture any urine the dog expels. For females, there is a similar urine-catching device that looks like a pair of britches with a hole for the dog's tail. Keep the appropriate device on your dog until the problem resolves. Guarding devices often help discourage marking as well as prevent it. It may be that some dogs don't like the wet against their body when they attempt to mark; also, not succeeding in leaving a scent may help discourage the action. If you find that your dog has a favorite place to mark, buy a dog repellant to help discourage him from marking in that place.

A belly band can help with marking issues.

Tethering your dog to you for retraining might also work. This technique requires you to keep your dog's leash attached to you so that he is never out of your sight. This allows you to use the leash to stop or interrupt his attempt to mark. Often, when tethered, a dog will not attempt to mark. When he isn't tethered, he should be put inside his crate. With the tethering technique, the marking behavior will often stop after a couple weeks.

When Marking Is Frustration Elimination

Sometimes a dog will mark immediately after someone leaves the house. This kind of marking is actually frustration elimination. I've known dogs who will also poop as well as pee in response to what resembles a kind of separation anxiety. Some dogs will both mark and engage in frustration elimination. Another reason why a dog may eliminate is when he's feeling insecure, especially when there is a change in the household.

One way to help control frustration elimination is to crate your dog when you leave. If he is reliable about not eliminating in the crate, it can help get your dog out of the bad habit. Crates, when used properly, can offer him a sanctuary and help insecure dogs feel secure. To make your dog feel secure in his crate, put him in it while you are home and keep him in the same room with you, either while you are working, watching television, or perhaps fixing dinner. Arrange it so that your dog can keep you in sight most of the time. Don't hesitate

Sometimes your dog will regress in housetraining because of stress

to move the crate from room to room when you move. Feeding your dog in the crate and giving him treats can also help build crate security. Toss a treat into the crate, let him eat the treat, and let him out shortly after he finishes it. Schedule a little one-on-one time when your dog is out of the crate. You'll need to counterbalance the time he's confined inside the crate with play and attention.

Stuart Eliminated Inside When He Was Frustrated

Velma acquired Stuart, a Pomeranian-Poodle mix, when he was a year and a half old. There was a litany of complaints about

Sometimes dogs with poor bladder control will pee when excited, such as when greeting.

suspected variation of separation anxiety. Some dogs will eliminate if their owners go outside for just a few minutes—even when other people are inside the house. It isn't unusual for a frustrated dog to eliminate on specific items, such as his owner's bed. Stuart's frustration seemed a result of too little time with his owner and too many attempts at negative discipline.

First, Velma had Stuart neutered. She then enrolled him in a basic obedience class with an instructor who used positive techniques and who understood how to teach good dog manners and how to teach a dog to look to his owner for guidance. Stuart quickly learned how to behave better and quickly bonded with Velma.

Velma cleaned her carpets with a product to get rid of pet odors. She also used the product on all areas that Stuart had marked inside the house—including walls and pieces of furniture. In a few areas that Stuart seemed most fond of marking, she applied a commercial dog repellent. She also put a belly band on Stuart, which prevented him from leaving his scent in the house. At first, Velma tried to use the belly band intermittently but found that this didn't work. She finally realized that she needed to be consistent with the use of the device. She also began crating Stuart when she wasn't home. Some dogs will accept being left home alone after six months to a year of crating and can be let out of the crate during the day. With other dogs, keeping them crated is the best solution.

Stuart found an owner who was willing

Stuart, the worst of which was he wouldn't housetrain. Stuart's prior owner's busy schedule left him little time for the dog, and the dog's lack of training made his owner want to spend even less time with him.

Stuart's housetraining issue wasn't so much that he didn't understand what was expected of him but was a result of him being frustrated. Dogs who are frustrated often eliminate shortly after their owners leave the house, making this issue a to spend more time with him and who was willing to get him some basic training and not use punishment. Velma's commitment and hard work paid off, and now she and Stuart are a happy family.

Submissive and Greeting Peeing

Few things seem to upset people more than submissive or greeting peeing. A submissive pee usually happens when you reach out to pet a dog. A greeting pee usually happens when you first arrive home and not necessarily when you are bending over to pet the dog. Both typically begin during adolescence. If handled correctly, submissive peeing will resolve by a year or a year and a half of age. If not handled correctly, you might own the problem for the life of your dog. Greeting peeing can be curbed by training and preventing the actions that precipitate the behavior.

Submissive Peeing

Although it may look like a defiant act, submissive peeing is actually a "gift" from

With submissive peeing, you must train your dog how to react to you without engaging in this behavior.

your dog. He's telling you that he sees you as his unquestioned leader. Never yell at your dog for submissively peeing. It doesn't tell him to stop—it tells him that he hasn't done a sufficient job submitting to you, leaving him with the option of trying all the harder. This may cause him to try to submit more acceptably by peeing *more* often!

To help with submissive peeing, you must first refuse the behavior. To do that, break any eye contact, stop any attempt to touch your dog, and walk away. This will tell him that you won't accept his "gift" of groveling. Second, you must begin training your dog how to react to you without peeing. He will have to learn how to accept affection without offering submission. After you walk away from your dog—your way of refusing the submissive gift—sit on the floor (if he's small) or on a chair (if he's large), and call him over. By petting your dog at his level and by not looming over him, he will often accept the attention without offering submission. If your dog still wants to approach you submissively by crawling

with a lowered head and tail, distract him out of that posture with a treat. I like to use a biscuit that is hard enough so that it isn't readily chewed. While your dog is crunching on the biscuit, pet him by first reaching toward his chin, then tracing your fingers along his jaw and up behind the ears. Finally, you can pat him on the head. This is the best technique for petting a submissive dog and will help put him at ease. When handled correctly, a dog will outgrow submissive peeing, and you will eventually be able to more directly approach him.

Greeting Peeing

Greeting peeing is not the same as submissive peeing. Although both often start when a dog reaches adolescence, greeting peeing can be tied into physical factors such as poor bladder control. Throughout their lives, some dogs have a hard time controlling their bladders when excited, while others manage to outgrow this problem.

Never punish or scold a dog who loses urine when excited because this will only complicate the problem. Instead, work to control the issue. If you have a dog who loses urine when he's excited, learn to de-emphasize your arrival home. Don't stop to pet him right when you get inside the door, and don't speak in a high, excited tone of voice. Instead, ignore your dog—don't make eye contact, and don't offer any attention.

If your dog has a lot of trouble holding his urine, you might want to take him to the door you use to take him outside to do his business. You may be able to use a treat to lure him to the exit rather than call him. Keep the treat moving until you get him outside. Once you've settled down in the house, let your dog in without paying him any attention. Go to a chair or couch and sit down. Only acknowledge or pet your dog if he approaches you calmly. If he isn't calm, turn your head to the side and ignore him.

When people come over to visit, put your dog outside or in his crate until the visitors have settled in. Explain to newcomers how to greet your dog—ask them not to bend over to pet him or make a fuss over him or use an excited greeting. The best way to let your dog greet new people is when they are sitting down. Ask your guests to sit quietly and pet him only if he approaches calmly.

Doogie Had Both Problems

Doogie, a chocolate Labrador Retriever, had a high drive to please and was committed to doing his owner's bidding. His owner, Mark, was unknowingly cuing him for some unwanted behaviors. Mark's tall and powerful stature caused him to naturally loom over his dog while petting him. Doogie, an overachiever, went out of his way to submit and began to submissively pee.

To solve the problem with submissive peeing, Mark changed his behavior and stopped looming over his dog. Instead, he sat in a chair and let Doogie come over to be petted. Because Mark was no longer accidentally signaling for Doogie to submit, he quickly stopped the behavior. Plus, as Mark worked on bonding and teamwork with his dog, Doogie learned to be comfortable with Mark and respond better.

Although Doogie resolved his submissive peeing issues, he still had issues with greeting peeing.

Mark and any guests began greeting Doogie calmly, or sometimes Mark would crate him until the house settled down, a measure he found worked well. Mark confessed that sometimes someone would pop over unexpectedly and greet Doogie the wrong way, and then there'd be a mess. But Mark is handling the issue in the correct way, and there's a chance that Doogie might outgrow it.

Looming over your dog may cause a submissive peeing response.

ChapterEleven

Help for Troubled Dogs:

Barking, Biting, Aggression, and Guarding Issues

This chapter includes information and guidance for some aggression problems, along with issues associated with barking, growling, and biting. Trying to resolve these problems is essential— aggression, especially, is a problem that must be addressed to prevent injury to a person or another dog. Seek the professional help of a behaviorist or experienced trainer for serious problem behaviors. A professional can help with management techniques and will analyze your dog for any unique problems.

Barking

Dogs bark to communicate. A bark may indicate a desire to play or a message to other dogs. Some dogs will bark when left at home to communicate frustration. Sometimes an older dog will take up barking as a result of senility. Some dogs bark when doing their job, such as a herding dog when working sheep, a terrier when flushing quarry, or a guard dog when protecting his territory. Some dogs bark to get attention or when they are excited or bored. These kinds of barking seldom end with the dog biting, although an excited dog may sometimes nip. Some dogs bark when they are afraid, and this fear may escalate to an aggressive level, where they will attack or defend themselves by biting.

Before trying to stop your dog from barking, you must first understand *why* he is barking. In cases where barking is a warning of aggression, you need to resolve the aggression, not the warning signs of aggressive behavior (the barking). However, if your dog is merely nuisance barking, you can resolve the issue through training.

Dogs bark to communicate.

Nuisance Barking

Barking isn't bad when it's done for the "right" reasons, and as dog owners, we need to define what "right" means and then train our dogs to follow suit. When deer are in my yard in the middle of the night, I don't want my dog to bark. However, if a coyote is by the chicken pen, I very much want my dog to bark. When a dog barks for reasons we don't want, we consider it nuisance barking.

Training the Quiet Command

As with all training, the best way to stop an unwanted behavior is to first train your dog to do what you want rather than punish what you don't want. To teach your dog to stop barking, first train him to stop barking on command. Typically, it is a good idea to acknowledge what your dog is barking at and give a little praise, then work to teach him to be quiet and reward that behavior with both praise and a treat.

1. Have several treats ready.
2. Have a volunteer come to the door and wait for your dog to start barking.

3. Acknowledge what he is barking at and give a little praise—remember, your dog feels that this is an issue that needs to be brought to your attention.
4. Say "Quiet," then toss a treat.
5. Toss out treats one at a time and repeat the word "quiet." (Eating the treats will help prevent him from returning to his task of barking.)

If your dog is not willing to comply with a *quiet* command when offered a treat, there are a few more things you can try to enforce your command.

Upping the Stakes Using a Spray Bottle

Although using a spray bottle to discourage unwanted barking is negative reinforcement, sometimes using something a little negative can be helpful in this case. If you've exhausted other techniques and the nuisance barking is making your (and your neighbors') life miserable, the spray bottle technique can help with this problem without resorting to harsher methods.

Step One

1. Fill a spray bottle with water.
2. Hide the spray bottle behind your back until your dog begins barking.
3. Time the spray of the mist so that he feels it on his face at the same time he hears you say "Quiet."
4. The unexpected feel of the water on his face should stop the barking.

Upping the Stakes

For some dogs, using a spray bottle to deter barking is too negative, while for others, this technique may be fine. Chapter 6: Upping the Stakes will help you find the right kind of correction for your dog. Upping the stakes allows you to start out very softly and then increase the consequences for noncompliance until the dog decides to reform. Although it would be nice if all dogs decided that a treat was all they needed to change a behavior, it just doesn't always work. What also doesn't work is using harsher training techniques than the dog needs. That is why it is important to start with a reward and work your way into consequences for noncompliance.

5. Repeat this timing a few more times until your dog associates the consequences of the spray bottle with the word "quiet."
6. Remember to keep the bottle hidden.

Step Two

Once your dog understands the consequences of not listening to your *quiet* command, give him the chance to comply before using the negative reinforcement.

1. Keep the spray bottle hidden behind your back.
2. Say "Quiet" when your dog begins barking, then give him a moment to comply.
3. If he doesn't comply, bring the bottle

from where you've hidden it behind your back and spray his face.

4. Repeat the word "quiet" at the same time the mist hit your dog's face.

Once your dog gets the idea that you will enforce your request to be quiet, often just using the word will bring compliance. However, with a dog who doesn't want to comply, you may have to state the *quiet* command and then hold up the bottle as a reminder that you can enforce this request. If your dog then chooses not to comply, carry through with the consequences of spraying the water.

Husher Device

If you've worked to train your dog to obey the *quiet* command using the reward method and then the spray method, your next step might be to look into a Husher. A Husher is a device that prevents a dog from barking by using elastic panels to encircle his snout. Although the Husher looks like a cloth muzzle, it won't stop a dog from biting because the elastic allows the mouth to open so that he may breathe and pant. The company that makes it states that it can be worn for long periods because the dog can eat or drink with it on, but some sources warn that this isn't true. If you do decide to use this device, don't leave your dog alone with it on. After a while, just like with the spray bottle, you may only need to hold up the device as a warning of consequences when your dog refuses to comply with your *quiet* command.

Discouraging Barking When You Are Not Home

Corrections for deterring barking need to be timely and consistent to provide adequate discouragement. When owners are not at home, they often turn to correctional devices to stop unwanted barking. The two main types of antibark collars currently on

Don't just start with discouragement techniques to help stop nuisance barking.

the market are the citronella collar and electronic shock collar. (Ultrasonic collars work the same as shock collars.)

The citronella collar has a plastic unit filled with citronella attached to the collar. When a microphone detects noise, a spray of citronella is emitted. Citronella is derived from lemongrass, a harmless herb, and the smell of it works to distract the dog. The collar is not hard to keep adjusted in the correct position as long as it is not too tight.

An electronic shock collar unleashes a shock triggered by vibrations instead of noise and scented spray like the citronella collar. Although one might guess that the electronic collar works better for keeping a dog quiet, a study by Cornell University showed that the citronella collar actually performed better. With the citronella collar, seven out of nine owners reported a decrease in barking activity. For users of the electronic collar, half of the participants reported no success with the collar. I don't recommend this type of harsh punishment device for nuisance barking.

Start Out Softly

Don't just start with discouragement techniques to help stop nuisance barking. Instead, try to figure out why your dog is barking and then up the stakes starting with the gentlest of methods. I knew of a woman who learned this lesson the hard way. Her seven-month-old male Belgian Tervuren would bark in his crate during dog shows.

Growling

Growling doesn't have one meaning. Some dogs growl as a warning, while others growl when they're playing or merely to express an opinion. Some dogs may be in the habit of growling, and when that behavior isn't dealt with correctly, they move on to biting or even an attack. A dog who intends to bite may growl as a warning before he bites or may growl at the same time he launches into a bite—or he may not growl at all before he bites. The bite that follows a growl may range from a nip to a serious bite that breaks the skin.

There is a false belief that correcting a dog who is growling is the best way to stop biting. Although this may work in certain situations, merely correcting a growl is no guarantee you will change his mind about biting. If your dog does not understand that he must stand down, all you are teaching him is to not signal before he attacks, which will result in him going straight to biting without giving a warning.

First she tried spraying him with water, and then she tried a citronella collar. Both failed. Finally, after watching him for a while, she realized that he was barking defensively. She started using distractions for her dog when he barked, getting him to look at her and then rewarding him with a treat for being quiet. That solved the problem.

Nipping and Biting

Ever wonder why dogs bite? A lot of people assume that only dominant dogs bite; however, biting is part of a dog's culture. Dogs will bite to defend territory or to stop want unwanted behavior, such as pestering from another dog, a littermate, or a person (especially a child). A dog will also bite when he's afraid or in pain. Sometimes he will bite to stop someone from hurting him or if someone is doing something that worries or frightens him. Many dog owners witness this kind of response when they attempt to clip their dog's nails. The dog may not like it or may be frightened, so he bites to stop the person from doing the unwanted behavior.

Some dogs use biting or nipping when they're doing their jobs. Terriers nip and bite their quarry to drive it from its den, and a herding dog will nip the heels of an animal to get it to move. These dogs are quicker to bite and nip with people in a matter-of-fact way unless they are trained not to bite.

A dog may bite to assert himself as well. That kind of action can mimic what some people do with a small child. A parent might tell a child several times to stop an action. If the child doesn't stop, the parent may go over and give a little swat. Dogs can assert themselves in a similar manner.

Usually puppies learn to inhibit their nipping when playing with littermates.

Age-Related Nipping and Biting

Puppies learn to gauge how hard to bite when playing with littermates. Too hard a bite will stop the play—an important lesson all puppies need to learn. If a puppy is taken out of a litter too early, he may not understand how hard to use his teeth when playing, and the task of educating him falls into the hands of his owner.

Adolescence can bring on biting issues because some individuals at this age can flip from frightened to very assertive. When searching for his place in the pack, a young dog may take up the biting habit as a way to test his boundaries. That's why obedience training is so helpful at this age—it's a way to teach him boundaries. Even if it's only practicing *sit*, *down*, and *stay*, it will remind your dog that you are in charge and he needs to comply. Adolescence is also where some dogs begin to guard food and possessions, and they will need to be trained to surrender food and toys on command.

Although a few adult dogs have biting or nipping issues as a carryover from unresolved adolescent issues, typically when an adult dogs bites, it's a serious situation. Sometimes it starts with a warning growl that is ignored or not resolved, then progresses when a more assertive dog decides to assert himself. Dogs who become overly protective and who are not trained to stand down by their owners may begin to bite people outside of the household. These unwanted bites can not only alienate friends and cause potential harm but can have legal repercussions. See "Aggression"

to help understand why a dog may begin to bite, and get professional help immediately, before it's too late.

Stopping Nipping in Puppies

The following is a series of techniques to stop a younger dog who bites. If you are dealing with an adult dog who bites as a result of aggression, you must resolve the underlying aggression issue to stop the biting. Seek professional help in that case.

Step 1

When your puppy mouths or bites you, say "Ouch" very sharply and then walk away. This will communicate to him that he hurt you and also that when he bites, playtime will end.

Stop playtime when your puppy starts to nip.

Gentle Leader as a Deterrent for Aggressive Dogs

A fellow dog trainer first introduced me to the Gentle Leader. She used it on an adolescent terrier named Picker, who bit his owner during training exercises. Actually, Picker would bite anyone who tried to get him to do anything. I asked her how she managed to get the Gentle Leader on Picker without getting bitten, and she explained that she put the dog on a table small enough and high enough that he had to worry about falling off that table. While he was preoccupied, she slipped the Gentle Leader on him.

This device may take a dog's aggressive tendencies down a notch. He still needs obedience and leadership training to resolve aggression issues, but this is a good way to approach problems with dog-to-dog aggression and dog-to-people aggression that haven't gotten too out of control. If you want to try the Gentle Leader, don't hesitate to do so under the guidance of a good dog instructor or behaviorist who has experience using the device correctly.

Step 2

If the "ouch" method fails, use a sharp "no" when he bites, then put your puppy in a crate for a 15-minute time-out. When working to retrain biting issues with a younger dog, many repetitions are often required.

Step 3

You may be able to divert your puppy's chomping urges toward an appropriate toy or Nylabone instead of your fingers.

Step 4

If your puppy persists with nipping, use your fingers to press gently on his muzzle and say "No bite." This is not meant to be a harsh reprimand but a correction. Do not squeeze your puppy. Hold the muzzle for about five seconds the first time and longer each successive time. Although I don't use a lot of corrections I see dogs use on each other, I like this one. I saw a mother dog use this on a rather rambunctious puppy. This particular puppy took quite some time to bring under control, but the mother dog persisted until her puppy finally quit. This kind of action can actually work to calm some puppies down. But remember, be gentle with your fingers.

Stopping Mouthing in Adults

When working with a mouthy adult who chomps on your hand uncomfortably but isn't aggressively biting, try the following steps. Keep in mind that adult dogs with biting issues need more than to be taught to stop the biting; they require professional help and good leadership training.

Step 1

First, try all the steps for puppies described earlier.

Step 2

Just as with nuisance barking (see "Barking"), you might want to try the spray bottle method. Say "No" when your dog nips or mouths too hard, and then say "No" again at the same time you spray the water.

Step 3

Place a few drops of Tabasco sauce (don't get it in your eyes) or lemon juice on your hands if you anticipate your dog mouthing you. Dogs typically don't like the taste, which can discourage him from doing it again.

Step 4

Try using a Gentle Leader, the training tool described in Chapter 4, if your dog

Some dogs, especially herding breeds, will try to bite you when you run.

nips. The first time or two, he will typically remain occupied trying to get the device off. If he persists in nipping, pull on the Gentle Leader's tab for about five seconds, then release. Say "No" at the start of the pull upward. Repeat twice if he persists, then give him a time-out in the crate. Don't pull to hurt your dog, but pull to interrupt him and divert his attention from nipping. When you let go, ask him to do something else, like sit. Pet him if he will allow you to without mouthing. If he again goes back to mouthing, repeat your message with a pull on the Gentle Leader. You may find that some dogs choose to sit when you pull on the tab. This action can be rewarded with affection as long as the mouthing isn't happening.

The Gentle Leader has a proven calming effect on dogs. Dr. Anderson, a veterinarian who worked on the creation of this device, explains that the Gentle Leader touches several pressure points on a dog's head that affect the sympathetic nerve system. Pulling on the tab is not meant as a reprimand but to interrupt an unwanted behavior. Once your dog has a chance to break his focus on what you don't want him to do, redirect to a behavior you want and then reward.

Nipping When You Run

Some dogs, especially herding breeds, will try to bite you when you run. As mentioned later in the aggression section, prey drive can initiate this behavior in dogs. Although all dogs have some prey drive, herding breeds tend to have more of an intense prey drive bred into them. The prey drive can result in a dog grabbing at his owner's hand, clothing, or heels when she runs.

If your dog has this drive, try to refocus his urge to nip at you. If he likes to chase a ball, throw it a few times to get him focused on it. Then start running a short distance, and throw the ball while you are moving. This will redirect your dog from trying to nip at you to focusing on the ball. If he tries to grab the ball out of your hand when you run, give a firm "No," and the next time, run a shorter distance before you throw the ball. Or you can try running with a device that holds the ball out at the end of a plastic stick. Once your dog learns to change his focus from you to something else (like the ball), build up in distance for running before throwing the ball. Then finally, start fading the use of the ball.

You can also try giving your dog something to hold in his mouth before you start running. Let him take hold of an object, such as a ball, and then start to run. This can help get your dog out of the habit of grabbing at something when he runs.

Aggression

Aggression in dogs can vary. Not only are there many different types of aggression (discussed in the following sections), but individual dogs can run the gamut from totally nonaggressive to severely aggressive. Severe aggression, where people are at risk of serious injury, requires the help of a behaviorist or trainer who works directly with the dog owner to resolve his issues. Do not hesitate to get such help when dealing with any type of aggression.

Assertive Aggression

Some assertive dogs may become aggressive if not trained to comply with their owners' commands. These dogs may turn to biting to assert themselves.

Dealing With Assertive Aggression

You need to train a more assertive dog to not make certain decisions without your guidance, especially if he bites to assert himself. If you fail to train this kind of dog, you or someone else can get hurt. The solution to this problem is not discipline but training and good leadership. You don't need to use choke chains, harsh reprimands, or discipline to reform this kind of dog. Start by using good leadership training, which is built by doing the power training found in Chapter 5. If you are working to resolve aggression issues with your dog, don't hesitate to enlist the help of a professional; however, find a dog behaviorist who understands how to use leadership training to reform aggression issues.

Dominance Aggression

Dominant dogs use biting to assert their dominance. It's a natural thing for a dog to do. Unfortunately, often the members of the dog's human family are the victims of this kind of aggression. Snapping when an owner tries to get her dog to move off a couch or biting if an owner tries to force

Resource Guarding

Although a more dominant dog typically guards his food, toys, and bed, dogs who are less dominant may also guard these resources. Many times, dogs who are not as dominant will bite to protect their possessions.

her dog to obey a command are signs of dominance aggression. Some dogs with dominance aggression issues may attack another dog in the household if the dominant dog sees the other dog getting too much attention. Dominant dogs are also more likely to bite to protect territory.

Canine dominance aggression typically develops at social maturity, which usually occurs between 18 and 36 months of age. However, some individuals may show signs as young as eight weeks. Both males and females can be dominant aggressive. In a household where the dog's owner has poor leadership, a more dominant dog may use aggression as a way to discover his boundaries, by possession guarding, controlling sleeping areas, and controlling which strangers or dogs can occupy the household. Dogs may show dominance aggression differently toward different family members, with children often being the most vulnerable.

A dog showing dominance who doesn't see his owner as the leader will often take charge and uses aggression to manage his power. Intact males are much more likely to be a problem; however, females and neutered males can also become problems. Some females will move up in pack status after they've whelped a litter and may become more dominant. Some dogs don't immediately take charge until after they gain enough of a leadership role, and then they begin to assert themselves. Often this can manifest as a bite to a household member whom the dog feels has gotten out of line. Dominance aggression can quickly grow to an unmanageable point in more assertive dogs and more confident breeds, as well as in guard breeds.

Dealing With Dominance Aggression

As with any form of aggression, seek professional help. Below are some methods I've found that can help with dominance aggression.

Obedience Training

Obedience training is a must when dealing with dominance aggression. Basic

If you find your dog showing signs of aggression, get professional help.

Good and Bad Help for Aggression

One of the saddest stories I know concerns some owners who sought professional help for their French Bulldog's aggression problems. At a year and a half of age, Charcoal began to bite the two children in the household when they tried to get him to move off the couch. The family had never trained him, and over time, this spoiled dog had taken command. A professional dog trainer was called in to help. The dog trainer showed the family how to pinch Charcoal's ear when he growled and then throw him into a crate. The dog trainer also taught the family to use an alpha roll.

Unfortunately, like many Bulldogs, French Bulldogs are not only dominant but sensitive as well. After a few months of this harsh treatment, Charcoal severely bit both kids. Also unfortunate was the fact that the harsh treatment recommended by the trainer had created a terrible problem. Charcoal now behaved much like a dog suffering from post-traumatic stress disorder and was at times unpredictably aggressive. Although he could have been saved in the right hands, there are not enough skilled people to reform a dog who has suffered this kind of damaging abuse. Often, a dog who is traumatized may need strong support and a lot of tolerance. These dogs seldom recover enough to be rehomed with a regular family. Unfortunately, there isn't always room for one more reformed dog at the skilled behaviorist's home.

obedience such as heeling and sitting and lying down on command give a foundation for control. However, because a dog typically gauges how much status and control he has based on privileges he commands, you need to do more than basic training. Your dog will need training to learn to relinquish control of any privileges that belongs to the leader of the pack. Training him to move from any sleeping area on command, give up food or toys when asked, and not demand affection are all necessary. Much of the power training discussed in Chapter 5 covers these issues and helps owners establish a leadership position.

Security in a Controlled World

Dominant dogs tend to want a very controlled environment, and if they don't have it, will automatically step up to take charge. Although one would expect a more dominant dog to be very secure, some seem to become stressed trying to control the entire world. It isn't unusual for a dominant dog to turn to aggression out of fear, which is later discussed in "Dealing With Fear Aggression." Dominant dogs typically feel more secure about their environment when their owners show strong leadership. This can take the pressure and stress off the dogs.

Fear Aggression

Fear aggression is the response a dog has when he feels threatened. Although some fearful dogs will run and some will cower, a dog with aggressive tendencies will bite. It isn't unusual for these dogs to be low in pack status and lack confidence. Because any perceived threat can solicit a bite, these dogs require a lot of confidence building and socialization.

Dealing With Fear Aggression

Owners who show strong leadership will often find that a fearful dog will learn to trust them in questionable situations that might otherwise frighten him to the point of biting. Likewise, owners who demonstrate poor leadership tend to have dogs who don't trust them and who resort to defending themselves. Once a fearful dog begins to bite to defend himself, the habit must be corrected. Simply muzzling your dog isn't a long-term answer because just stopping the action is not enough—he needs to learn how to feel secure. In fact, muzzling a fear biter and not solving the underlying issue

Genetics Has a Role in Aggression

Certain lines of dogs can have more aggressive individuals. I've known people who bred a more aggressive terrier for hunting, thinking that trait was the key to a good hunting dog. But what really makes a good hunting dog is a high prey drive and intelligence, not aggression. However, many people misunderstand the purpose of aggression in a dog. The same problem can occur with people who breed pit bull crosses for a higher degree of aggression, hoping to create the ideal "guard dog." A good guard dog only uses aggression as a tool. Dogs who are not in control of their aggression become killers, not good guard dogs.

can make him neurotic because he will feel trapped and unable to defend himself. Punishing a fearful dog for biting will also do nothing to solve the issue.

Unfortunately, fearful dogs often require extensive work with a professional and may always need protection from what they perceive as an overwhelming situation.

Frustration Aggression

People who are prevented from achieving a goal may end up frustrated, and that frustration can turn to aggression—this is called frustration aggression. With people, the closer they get to a goal, the greater the excitement and expectation, which results in more frustration when they are held back. Researchers studying aggression in dogs noticed that dogs who were not allowed to interact "naturally" with other people and other dogs showed a similar kind of aggression. Often, a barrier of some kind, such as a leash, fence, or window, prevented the dog from a natural interaction. Researchers observed that the longer a dog was physically restricted from the interaction, the more intense his desire was to gain access to what he wanted. Dogs in this situation became increasing excited, agitated, or frustrated, and that agitation and frustration sometimes turned into aggressive behavior.

Some leash aggression is suspected to be frustration aggression. Also, confinement behind a fence can lead dogs who don't even have a guard drive to escalate their aggression. One indicator that a barrier is creating frustration is if your dog is calm and friendly around other dogs or people when not restricted by a fence or a leash. Other factors in frustration aggression are improper socialization and too little exercise.

Too little exercise is a factor in frustration agression.

The best way to prevent frustration aggression is to avoid putting your dog in a situation that may trigger him. Observe your dog when he's outside in the yard (especially if the yard is by a road), and see if he becomes frustrated when people, dogs, bikes, or cars go by. If he runs along the fence and barks at any of these stimuli, take him out of this situation, as it will just escalate if left alone. Some dogs may even become so frustrated that they redirect their aggression to someone or something in the yard.

Leash Aggression—a Type of Frustration Aggression

Leash aggression, where a dog lunges and tries to attack another dog, can occur when he is insecure. Some dog trainers suspect that this is a variation of territory aggression or that it's created by frustration aggression. Often, dogs who are left tied outside will display a similar aggression.

When working to correct leash aggression, severe jerking and harsh corrections do more to fuel the aggression than to curb it. Some people who have tried to use a stiff

Leash aggression may be a variation of territory aggression.

jerk on the leash once their dog is actively lunging, snapping, and barking have had their dog turn and bite them (known as redirected aggression).

- To be effective when correcting leash aggression, begin working with your dog at a distance from another dog where he still feels comfortable.
- Watch for your dog to raise his head, stare at the other dog, or stiffen his posture—this is the time to intervene and work to redirect his attention.
- Pull your dog's leash to move his head and break his focus; sometimes you may need to turn in a small circle to get him to look away.
- Once you break his attention from the other dog, use a treat to redirect your dog's attention to you.
- Get him to relax, even if you need to amble away from the dog that is concerning your dog.

Retraining a dog with leash aggression can take a lot of work, but he can learn to relax around other dogs.

An Insecure Dog Who Relaxed as We Talked

One day while out on a walk with my dogs, I passed by my neighbor, Ellen, who had just adopted a two-year-old Australian Shepherd named Parker. Ellen had already begun Parker on obedience work, and the dog was following along her side nicely until he got about 30 feet (9 m) away from us. Then, Parker noticed my two dogs. He immediately pulled back against his leash, and when the slack was gone, he thrashed and gave a higher-pitched bark than normal. When Ellen tried to walk closer to us, Parker lunged forward and snapped at my dogs.

Ellen stopped Parker a short distance away and worked to calm him down by using some of the obedience commands she'd practiced. He finally quit lunging at my dogs and stood behind her. We waited for about ten minutes, and during that time, Parker (a more sensitive dog) picked up on Ellen's calm demeanor. Because we stood in the same place and did not try to force him to go any closer to my dogs, he had the chance to settle down and relax. To our surprise, Parker seemed to pick up on our relaxed and friendly tone and decided that my dogs were no longer a threat. The dogs actually sniffed each other, which was a big step for her insecure dog.

Many insecure dogs are also very in tune with their owner's emotions. If you

Leave guard-dog training to professionals, like Alex Dunbar, seen here training a German Shepherd Dog for police work.

are having problems with fear-generated aggression, make sure that you are adding to your dog's sense of security by keeping a calm demeanor. Raising your voice to correct him, using a higher-pitched tone, or jerking on the leash will not build security. It's better to find a distance where your dog can settle down and reassure him by projecting a calm but strong attitude. Your dog will find your solid stance and self-assured attitude reassuring. Keep in mind that you don't want to baby him, as this will not help reassure him.

Guard Dog-Associated Aggression

Many insurance companies have a black list of "dangerous" dogs, which may include Rottweilers, Doberman Pinschers, and German Shepherd Dogs. If you own one of these breeds, you may face a higher premium or even be dropped because too many of these dogs have earned a reputation for aggression—usually biting. Often, the aggression is caused by the dog's guard-dog drive. Understanding the guard-dog drive and learning what specialized

German Shepherd Dogs used for police work are highly trained.

training is needed can help you teach a guarding breed to not bite unexpectedly.

Alex Dunbar, of Close Quarters Battle K-9, is an expert in guard-dog mentality because he raises and professionally trains German Shepherd Dogs for police work, the military, and personal protection. Alex explains that a good guard dog does not depend on excess aggression to do his job but is intelligent enough to be trained to distinguish a real threat from one that doesn't need to be acted on. His German Shepherd Dogs are bred with what he calls a "switch," which allows them to grab hold of the bad guy one moment and release that person and calm down on command. To train these guard dogs correctly, Alex does a lot of socialization from the time they are puppies. Dogs are then drilled on what to react to and when to react. They are also taught a command to stop the attack and assume an "at-ease" attitude.

Working With Guard Dogs and Guests

Dogs with a guarding drive need to be taught how to greet guests. A guard dog will want to protect the property and must learn that strangers coming into the house are fine. You can set up a training situation that will teach your dog that someone knocking on the door or ringing the doorbell is not a cue for him to go into guarding mode. If your dog goes into a guarding state of mind, he is more likely to bite someone.

You can teach your dog to relax when a guest arrives by beginning your training

with a family member he knows. Have the family member go outside. After your dog has settled down about the person's departure, have the family member ring the doorbell or knock on the door. When your dog begins to bark or give attention to the

Have a family member pretend to be a "guest" when teaching a guard dog how to greet people.

anticipated "intruder," tell him it's okay in a calm voice, and get him to quiet down by asking for a *sit* or a *down*, and then have him look at you (the *watch* command). Once he settles down, let the family member come in. Have the family member greet your dog in a calm way, pet him, and give him a treat so that he associates arrivals to the house with good things.

Practice this exercise until your dog gets used to settling down at the sound of the doorbell or someone knocking. Then, do the same practice session with a friend with whom your dog is familiar. Once again, have him settle down before the friend comes in. Have him make eye contact with you, then have the person greet him and give him a treat.

Ideally, you should progress to practicing the lesson with someone your dog doesn't know. When using someone he isn't as familiar with, keep an eye on your dog and make sure that he learns to relax as well as he did with a family member. Once he learns to accept strangers amiably, you'll still need to watch him when people come over. Certain people may trigger a guarding

Sighthounds often have high predatory drives.

The Maid Must Be Stopped!

"I have a three-year-old male Dachshund who has taken issue with the maid who comes weekly to clean my house. He goes crazy barking and trying to snap at her heels as she goes about the housework. She has never yelled at the dog or done anything to provoke him. How can I get him to accept my maid, and why does he hate her?"

There are two things that may precipitate this kind of behavior. First, the dog may be reacting to a triggered predatory drive. Dog breeds, such as Dachshunds, that were bred to work quarry in a den can be sensitive to certain household machinery. A vacuum may seem like an animal on the attack, and these breeds were bred to attack back. The dog may conclude that the maid needs to be dealt with before she attacks again.

Another possible issue is that the dog is frightened by the vacuum, and a frightened dog will either flee or fight. Because the maid is not part of the household, the dog may have an added urge to protect his territory. If a dog is upset and frightened even when the owner is the one vacuuming, the best solution is to crate him or put him someplace secure, away from the vacuum.

reaction in your dog. If you see him fixating on a guest or if his posture stiffens or his hackles go up, first try putting him in a *down-stay* and have him redirect his focus on you. If this doesn't succeed, put your dog in his crate. Don't let him continue to fixate on a guest.

Predatory Drive Aggression

Predatory behavior may be exhibited by dogs of any sex and age. All dogs have some level of predatory drive (prey drive), which is a part of their food acquisition behavior. Prey drive actions include chasing, pouncing, biting, pulling down another animal or object, shaking an animal or object in an attempt to kill it, rebiting, and carrying an object. This drive can show up as the motivation to chase anything that moves, including joggers, children, cats, bikes, and cars, or to catch and to kill small furry or feathered creatures. Prey drive is triggered more easily in some dogs and may even escalate from chasing and barking to aggression. The prey drive can even turn into a frenzy, with the dog losing all control. Dogs who escalate into aggression can also become fearful, which can compound the aggression problem. Some breeds are bred to use prey drive in their work and include herding breeds (German Shepherd Dogs, Belgian Tervurens, Border Collies); Rottweilers (who have some herding blood); hunting breeds like terriers (including Yorkshire Terriers!) and Dachshunds; and sighthounds (Greyhounds and Whippets).

Predatory Aggression Around Babies or Young Children

Predatory aggression can result in attacks on a crying baby or a child who is screaming or running. Some dogs who are bred to hunt experience an overwhelming urge to attack when an animal—even a human animal—sounds like it is in distress or pain. Dogs who are affected seem to go from a calm to frenzy-like state in an instant, with tragic consequences. With some dogs, specialized training and desensitization can help with predatory drive issues. However, the safest bet is to never allow this kind of dog with babies or children unless the dog is restrained or otherwise under control.

Watch your dog when he's outside to see if he has tendencies for territory aggression.

Territory Aggression

Territory aggression deals with a dog protecting property. That property can be anything from an owner's purse or jacket to the household boundaries. One dog owner thought it was cute when her dog growled at anyone who came near her purse. Although the idea that her dog loves her so much that he'd protect her purse is endearing, the behavior is a predecessor to problems. A dog can't be allowed to guard anything without strict guidance from his owner. Good guard dogs are specifically trained for their tasks. Part of the training entails taking guidance from a dog owner. Letting a dog chose what and when to guard can result in someone getting bitten.

When dogs make guarding decisions, they go by their set of rules and ideas. They decide when and if they should bite or if they should merely growl and bark. You don't want your dog deciding how much aggression to use because his idea of how to handle the situation probably won't coincide with what you really want. Unfortunately, sometimes dogs will become territorially aggressive when fenced inside a yard.

Dealing With Territory Aggression

The best way to deal with territory aggression is prevention. Although any dog can become overly protective of territory, guard dog breeds, such as Great Pyrenees, German Shepherd Dogs, and Doberman Pinchers, are especially prone.

The Sad Truth

Some people can work out problems with dog aggression and reform a dog to the level where he can once again safely interact with people. This process usually involves the help of an animal behaviorist who specializes in aggression issues. However, many times, there are too few experts to help or the dog owner can't commit the time or finances.

I wish all aggressive dogs could be saved, but too often there are too few people who can manage this problem once it takes hold. It is unforgivable to rehome a potentially dangerous dog without alerting the potential owner to his issues. Part of the responsibility of owning a dog includes making sure that he doesn't harm others. Some people find it easier to give away a potentially dangerous dog than to put him to sleep; no one ever wants to see a dog destroyed, but it is unethical to put someone else at great risk.

Don't leave your dog unattended in a fenced area until you have seen how he reacts to strangers walking by. If he barks at the fence at all—and especially if he lunges at the fence—then you need to monitor him and keep him on a leash when he's outside. Don't leave him outside all day if you can't watch him because you'll need to intervene if he decides that he must defend his territory.

Neutering

The most important thing to help with territory aggression is to get your dog neutered or spayed. Just as an intact male is more likely to mark his territory, he is also more likely to protect it. Studies have also shown that intact males, in general, are more aggressive than neutered males. The higher level of testosterone in an intact male is cited as a factor. Because dogs can form habits over time, neutering at a younger age—at about six months—helps prevent this issue.

Calling Down

Show strong leadership with a territorial dog. Get a professional to help you learn how to call down your dog when he is engaging in territory aggression. Usually, this is done by putting a dog on a long lead and having someone come by a fenced yard or other area where he tends to lunge or bark at a fence. When your dog lunges at the fence, don't make a comment—just use the leash to interrupt the unwanted behavior and then pull him back to you. When he is back by your side, ask him to settle down by having him sit. By not

Make sure your dog is mentally and physically stimulated.

Dogs who are underexercised may develop problem behaviors.

commenting when you interrupt the unwanted behavior, you're trying to communicate to your dog not to take this action, even when you are not around to call him down. If his intensity doesn't diminish after a few times, follow up with a sharp "No" at the same moment you engage the leash. Some dogs will back down with this technique. Some will only pause and will then again engage with territorial aggression.

If your dog wants to again take up the aggressive behavior, you may want to try putting on a Gentle Leader. This device has a calming effect with some dogs. After you

put on the Gentle Leader, try the training just mentioned, attaching the leash to the Gentle Leader to interrupt and redirect the unwanted behavior. Do this consistently with your dog until he abandons the unwanted behavior completely, not just for the one training session.

Exercise

Dogs who are underexercised and lack mental workouts are more likely to persist in territorial aggression. Make sure that your dog is mentally and physically stimulated by playing with him and going for walks.

Chapter Twelve

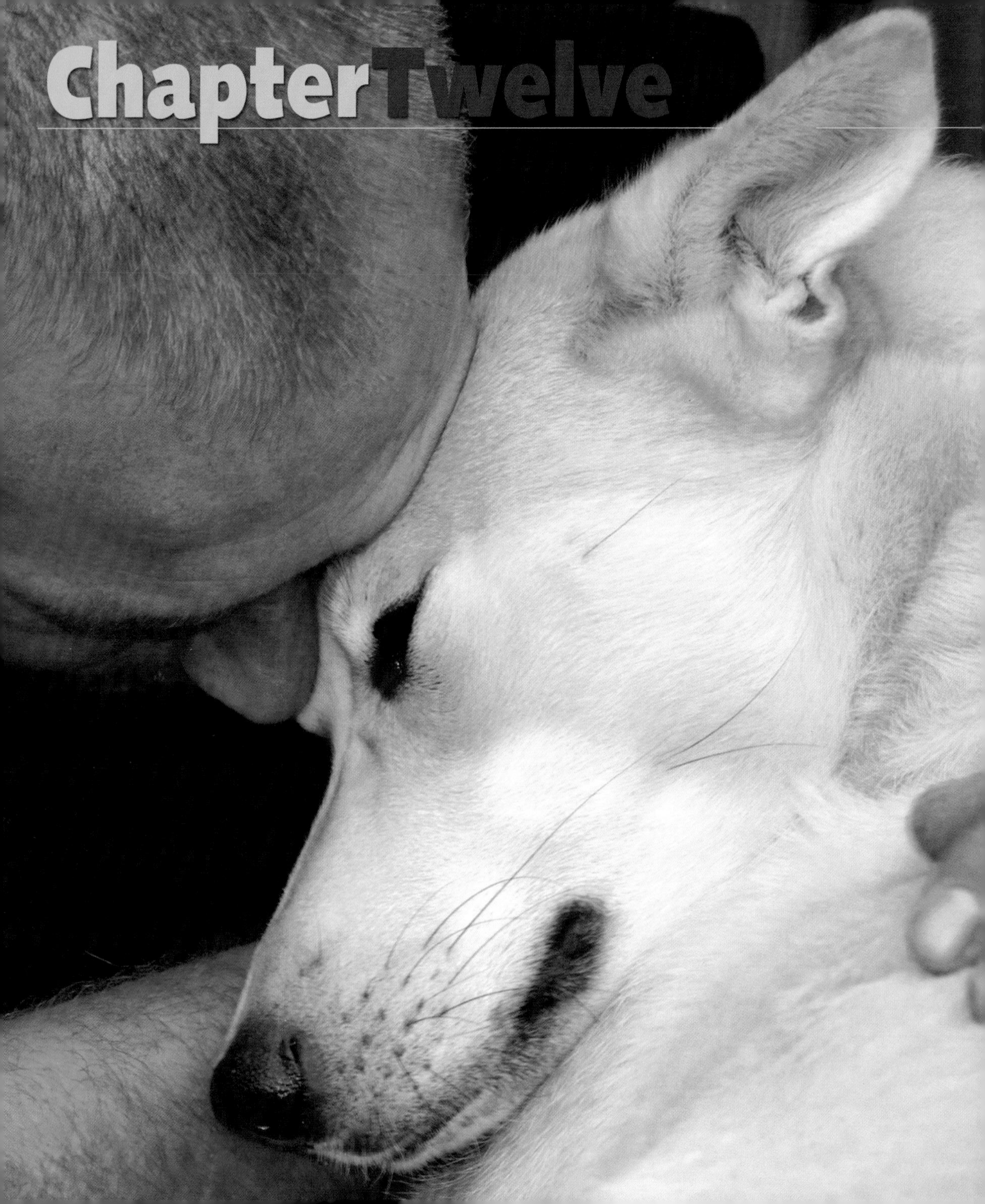

Case**Studies**

Below are two case studies of hard-to-train dogs. Max and Chamois both had issues, but luckily, they had owners willing to put in the time and effort to reform their dogs.

Max

Max, the Dog who Flunked Puppy Class and Almost Had Me for Lunch

I first met Max, an adolescent German Shepherd Dog, when our new neighbors were walking him along the road. Max was pulling against the leash and barking as I walked by. I asked his owners, Len and Dolly, to bring Max over so that I could give him an evaluation. Dolly explained that Max had been to a puppy class offered through a local pet-supply store. I asked them to show me what Max had learned to do. They commanded Max to sit about five times. Finally, Max planted his back end for an instant but then got right back up. He was far too distracted to comply for very long.

Having worked extensively with so many dogs who resist compliance, I expected the problem was that this dog didn't want to comply. But it turns out my diagnosis was wrong. After working with Max a little more and asking a few more questions, I discovered the real problem. He didn't fail puppy class—it was the puppy class that failed him. In my conversations with Dolly, I discovered that the instructor had no dog training experience and merely read instructions out of a notebook. In the meantime, other out-of-control puppies in the class kept coming over and distracting Max when Dolly tried to get him to do a command. By the time the class ended, instead of learning how to do basic commands, Max had learned how to become distracted when Dolly tried to work with him.

Basic Training Revisited

Max's reform began by having Dolly work on basic training. She trained in an environment with very few distractions—a quiet area inside her own home. Mastering the *sit* was first on the list. Because Max was only used to holding a *sit* for a moment, Dolly asked for the *sit*, then gave several treats, one after another, to keep Max in the position. When she was done, she gave a release word and walked away. It didn't take long before Max learned to sit still instead of getting right up. Next, Dolly worked on the *watch* command and then the *down*. She used a treat to teach Max to heel alongside her—and she did extra work with Max when teaching him to heel outside because there were so many more distractions.

Max's Guard Dog Drive Kicks In

Max had a drive to comply and did well once Dolly learned a few training techniques. A month later, I went over to see how things were going with Max. Dolly brought him outside to meet me. The moment Max saw me, he immediately stiffened his posture, his hackles went up, and he gave me a fixed stare. I'd seen this kind of stare from a dog trained and waiting for a cue to attack. Max was not trained to attack, but he was thinking about doing that very thing.

Some dogs have a natural urge to guard. This is usually seen in breeds that were originally bred for those traits, such as the Great Pyrenees, Doberman Pincher, and German Shepherd Dog. While not every individual dog of these breeds may have a strong guarding drive, both Max's sire and dam were Schutzhund (German for protection dogs) Champions. For a dog to do well in

Schutzhund, he must have a strong guard dog drive, which means that Max got those guarding genes.

Max responded to me as a possible threat for a couple reasons. First, his strong guard-dog drive gave him a natural urge to size up people and determine if he should take aggressive action. Second, Max was not very socialized. Because he didn't see many people outside of the house, he didn't have a lot of opportunity to know how to react to strangers. However, even with proper socializing, he still needed to be trained on how to respond to strong guarding instinct. As he fixated his stare on me, I could tell he was quite tempted to have me for lunch.

I stopped about 10 feet (3 m) away. In a calm voice, I asked Dolly to have Max sit. I then told her that he was fixating on me like a guard dog fixates on a person. She said that she'd noticed Max's body had stiffened when I approached and his hackles had risen. I had hoped that having Max sit would communicate to him that I was not a threat and he could relax, but Max needed more encouragement.

I was glad that Dolly had been doing her basic training with Max. I told her to ask Max to look at her. When he did, he relaxed and I could safely approach. Once Max decided that I wasn't a threat, he let me work with him on some training.

More Socialization Needed

Even though Dolly and Len bought Max to be a family pet, for him to be a dog who is safe around other people, they need to do a lot of work with him. Max needed a lot of socialization with children outside of their family and with people of all ages, sizes, and

Finding a Puppy Class

No matter where you go for puppy classes, there are a few things you should ask of the instructor:

- What are her credentials? Where I taught dog training classes, not only did the instructors need to have demonstrated training ability, we had to serve an internship.
- What kind of training techniques does the instructor use? If the instructor believes in forcing compliance instead of positive training techniques, find a different class.
- Does the trainer have experience in training your breed of dog? Many trainers are handy with dogs who are easy to trai, but not as good with the more challenging breeds. If the dog instructor already does a lot of training with challenging breeds, you will often fare better in the class.

demeanors. Dolly had taken the first necessary steps by doing basic training, but she needed to take Max to places outside the home to meet more people and other dogs. She started slowly and worked up to more and more human and animal interactions. Eventually, Max was able to meet and greet strangers without setting off his guarding drive.

Guard Dogs and Guests

Max also needed to understand how to greet guests who came to visit the family. We used the training method described in Chapter 11, in the section "Working With Guard Dogs and Guests," to help Max become reliable about meeting visitors to the home.

Case Studies

Chamois

Chamois, a Pleasant, Friendly, but Dominant Dog

Chamois (sounds like "Shammy") was a six-year-old Labrador and Golden Retriever mix. Wendy, her owner, got her as a puppy when she was eight weeks old. Chamois had already been trained on basic commands—she could sit when asked and knew how to stay, lie down, and fetch a toy. She'd even let her owners balance a treat on her nose.

Like most retrievers, Chamois was compliant, but she had a tendency toward dominance. Chamois already had a score book and was keeping track of which privileges she controlled and which she would relinquish to Wendy. Chamois would dominate play and also had taken charge as to which dogs could stay in the house and which could not. At one point, Chamois began to attack Wendy's small Miniature Pinscher mix and eventually injured her so badly that Wendy decided to rehome the Pincher mix. Chamois made this power move to get rid of the unwanted dog when she was about three years old. Dogs who want to claim privileges usually start around a year old. From one to four years, these dogs seem adamant about gaining power. After that, they work more on defending their privileges than on acquiring more.

Chamois took any and all power she could. This is not to say that she was a bad dog by nature, but her more dominant tendencies led her to power issues over playing and attention. When anyone tried to play catch with her, she would not relinquish the ball. She also didn't like to let go of toys when playing. When it came to getting attention, Chamois nudged and insisted on being petted. One time, when she was told to stay out of a room, she barged in and presented her stomach to a visitor to be petted. Although a submissive dog will present his tummy when people approach, a dominant dog may also do this. The difference is that the submissive dog will often roll to his back when people approach, while the dominant dog will do the approaching and will roll over, demanding attention.

One thing to keep in mind with a dominant dog is that the dog takes control bit by bit. That is the way an owner needs to take back control, a little at a time. An owner can't hand out a barrage of harsh punishment and have a reformed dog. Harsh punishment will come across as aggressive to the dog. In a pack, aggressive confrontations are typically used when the alpha wants to eject another animal from the pack.

To assert herself as the leader in Chamois' case, Wendy needed to regain control during play and control when her dog would receive attention.

Watch Me

With Chamois' retraining, I did the first part of the lesson to illustrate how the training was done, and then Wendy worked in the same fashion with her dog.

Round One

The first step was a short lesson on getting the dog to watch me for a treat. After a few practices, Chamois got the idea, but then she decided to try to get the treat on her terms—by barking at it. I ignored the barking and kept the treat held out until Chamois gave up and made eye contact. This lesson was the only lesson on the first training day. I wanted to allow her some time to think over the idea that I was going to take control, and give her a chance to launch a protest. Most dogs who have gained power will not readily give the status up without a protest.

The next lesson had several parts. The first part was to again practice making eye contact to earn a treat. Chamois did this twice, and then she again tried barking. She added pawing as she became more insistent that the treat be handed over on her terms and not mine. Again, any treat solicitation by Chamois was ignored, and I patiently waited until she gave up.

The next part of the lesson was to give a command and then tempt the dog to disobey. To bait Chamois into doing what she wanted over my request, I used a treat as a temptation. In preparation for this lesson, a 6-foot (2-m) leash was attached to Chamois' collar and a small piece of carpet set down so that we could make sure we had her sit in the same place each time. Because Chamois knew what "sit" and "stay" meant, she was asked to sit and to stay, which she did quite readily. A treat was then tossed a short distance away. Chamois immediately got up and went after the treat, but she didn't get very far because I had my foot on the leash. She looked a little confused when she was stopped in her attempt to get the treat I'd just tossed. I calmly asked her to again sit and stay. Then I waited. For a long time, Chamois sat on the small piece of carpet and stared at the treat as if doing so would get her what she wanted. Finally, she looked at me.

Choosing to Comply

It is very important to allow dominant, assertive, and independent dogs to try to achieve the training goal on their terms. They must be allowed to choose to comply and not be forced. The lesson they need to learn is that to get what they want, they must do what their owners want.

I immediately told her "Okay, go get it" and allowed her to get the treat.

Chamois was again asked to sit and stay on that small piece of carpet. When I tossed the treat, she again got up to get it but was stopped when she reached the end of the leash. This time, Chamois sat back down and stared at the treat without my having to request a *sit*. This told me she was very smart and quick to figure things out. Still, she didn't look at me for a while, even though she could easily figure out from her previous lesson that that was the way to receive permission to get the treat. Although some dogs may need time to learn what they need to do to earn a reward, in this case I suspected that Chamois was trying to figure out how to take charge and get things on her terms. Although she was quick to figure out that there was no use going after that treat when I tossed it, it took a few more practices before she decided to look at me right away for permission. Once we got one or two successes, the lesson was changed.

This time, Chamois was asked to lie down. Again she was told to stay and a treat was tossed. As with the *sit*, when Chamois went for the treat, the leash stopped her. I simply stood by looking as if I had little to do with the stopping action (although because I was standing on her leash, I had everything to do with stopping her). As far as Chamois was concerned, because I didn't yell or jerk on the leash, my ability to stop her from getting the treat seemed much more powerful than if I had given visual or verbal cues.

Once again I waited for Chamois to look at me before I gave her a release from her *down-stay* to get the treat. However, when I took her back to the small rug and requested her to lie down the second time, I ran into a little rebellion. Chamois sat down on the rug when I asked her to lie down, and then she stared at me as if she didn't understand what I meant when I had asked her to lie down.

I've had dogs not do a command before. Sometimes they are too distracted to hear my command, so I give the command again. But I knew that Chamois had heard me because of the tentative way she'd watched me. So I figured that this dog just didn't want to comply. The first thing I did was make sure that my posture was assertive by pulling back my shoulders and taking a solid stance. I didn't repeat my command but instead looked at Chamois while thinking "You don't have a choice—you are going to do this." I'm not mad when I think this, but I do feel assertive and sure of myself, and I believe that thinking those words gives me an expression on my face the dog can understand. My expression is not intimidating, but it does come across as calm and assertive. That kind of attitude will work to make a dog comply better than a threat will. Chamois decided after a few minutes to lie down. We again did the drill, but this time I also patted her for compliance because I know that she likes affection. The extra attention

also let her know that not only was I in control of the food, but I controlled the attention. The message I wanted her to understand was that when she did what I wanted, she'd get what she wanted, whether that was a treat or attention.

If Chamois hadn't lain down after several minutes, I would have repeated the command. If she still refused, I would have lured her down and then rewarded her for her compliance. If that didn't work, I'd have put her in a crate for a time-out, then brought her out and asked again. The last resort would be to enforce the command using the leash to stop her from getting up, and I'd only do that if I couldn't figure out any other way to achieve compliance. There is so much more to gain when you allow these dogs to choose to comply.

Because Chamois did comply and lie down, I only requested that she do a *down-stay* one more time, then moved on to the next issue I wanted to cover.

Round Two

Wendy kept up with the *watch me* lessons for a week before I returned to again work with her dog. Wendy noticed that Chamois seemed quite content to give a quick glance for a treat but wouldn't look for a long time. It isn't unusual for a dog to give a quick but minimal compliance glance with the *watch* command. At first, a quick look is fine, but for this exercise to be the most effective, the dog needs to learn to focus on the owner and not merely perform a token trick to receive a reward. Therefore, it is necessary for him to learn to watch longer and longer.

One way to do this is when your dog looks at you, don't say "Yes"; (which is an "end point," or final word) instead, say "Good." You can repeat "Good" each time he flashes a look and even drag out the word when he holds a look a little longer. Use the *good* command to acknowledge a glance. Do this about three times before saying "Yes" and then rewarding. Soon you can ask for more glances and longer glances. It isn't a bad idea to teach your dog to watch you for half a minute or more.

In this second lesson, I only practiced with Chamois once with the request for her to sit-stay while I threw a treat. She did it right the first time. Had she not, I'd have done this drill until she did it correctly before moving onto something new.

The next lesson was done just like the first, only instead of tossing a treat, I wanted to toss one of Chamois' toys because I knew that she had issues with taking control when playing. I didn't start with this lesson first because I wanted to work on something Chamois was less invested about controlling—the food treat. Had I begun by tossing a toy instead of a treat, I chanced getting a lot more immediate resistance from her. By starting with the food, I had the opportunity to work Chamois into the idea of giving up some of her control.

I put Chamois in a *sit-stay* and then tossed one of her squeaky toys. She not only immediately got up to pursue, but she did so faster and with more force than she had for the food. This wasn't a big surprise because Chamois showed a lot more enthusiasm for playing than she did for eating.

Chamois Rebels

The second time the toy was tossed, Chamois again tried to pursue but stopped when she reached the end of the leash. Although it took a moment, she finally sat down and then looked my way for a release. The third time I did this, Chamois would not go after the toy at all. It was as if she had decided that if she couldn't play on her terms, she wouldn't play.

There are a couple ways I deal with this kind of defiance. One is to put the dog up in a crate for a time-out and play with a second dog. The goal is to let the dog know what he is missing out on by not complying. However, because Chamois had previously shown aggressive jealousy with the Miniature Pinscher mix, I chose not to play with another dog in front of Chamois. Instead, I took the toy and used a high-pitched and excited tone of voice. I threw the toy and squeaked it and carried on until she decided to join in the action. I played with Chamois a few moments, then again asked for her to sit-stay and wait for a release. After Chamois complied once, I turned the lesson over to Wendy.

Chamois Shuts Down

After Wendy practiced with Chamois twice, Chamois shut down. When asked to lie down and stay, she did so; however, when the toy was tossed, instead of going to fetch it, Chamois laid down her head and began to mope. In defense of the dog, a mope isn't just a bad attitude that needs eliminated. Looking at the situation from Chamois' perspective, in a fairly short amount of time, we were asking her to give up a lot of leadership she had worked hard to secure. She was happy how things were going in the household and couldn't understand why Wendy was now determined to take away her coveted control.

When a dog mopes or sulks, you don't need to punish this action, nor should you reward it. I typically either walk away and ignore the dog

What Happens if the Leash Slips

During a training lesson, both Wendy and I had the leash slip out from under our foot when the toy was tossed and Chamois pursued. With me, I thought I was standing on the darn thing but wasn't. With Wendy, she didn't have shoes on, and the dog pulled hard when chasing the toy, which caused the leash to slip from under her foot. If this happens, merely go and get your dog and repeat the lesson the right way, as if nothing has gone wrong. By not emphasizing the mistake, your dog is more likely to focus on the right way to do things and not dwell on your mistake.

or find a way to break him out of the mope that doesn't involve punishment. Because Chamois broke out of the mope last time by offering some play, I again used an excited voice and a squeaky toy as a lure. I tossed the toy up in the air and caught it a few times while sounding very excited and happy. Then I offered Chamois the toy by shaking it in front of her. She finally joined in, at which time I played with and petted her. After a little playtime, she was asked to comply one more time. When she did, she was rewarded with more play and more attention. This was where the lesson ended.

Although this lesson was far shorter than the first, Chamois let us know that she'd had enough when she shut down. When a dog indicates he's had enough, you need to stop the training, but make sure that you are in a controlling position when you stop. Don't end at the point the dog mopes, but have him do something to comply. You don't need

to make him comply to whatever set off the adverse reaction. It is often better to change to a different request. Even a simple *sit*, if your dog does that readily, gives you a chance to end the lesson with you rewarding compliance, not stopping at a point where he has failed to comply. I have found that many dogs need to gradually work into more and more compliance. Part of the process involves breaking their old habits as well as teaching them that there is a reward in doing things your way. I have yet to find a one-lesson wonder technique that guarantees reform.

If you have a dog who is showing a lot of reluctance to reform, one way to help diminish this issue is to up the reward. Chamois didn't find treats nearly as rewarding as pets and playtime. With this dog, giving more playtime when she complied and petting her along with the playing was a good way to help motivate her. Keep in mind that a dog undergoing this kind of reform is giving something up. Chamois was quite content in the areas where she'd taken control. To help soothe her loss of power, it helped to offer a replacement, such as more affection and play, given as a direct reward for compliance.

More Work

Because retaking control is a slow process, Wendy began to ask Chamois to sit and then make eye contact to get her evening meal. This allowed Wendy a way to work every day to remind Chamois who was now in control. Wendy worked each evening, asking for longer and longer eye contact until Chamois went from that brief glance to a respectable stare.

Chamois also needed to learn how to let go of a toy when she had it in her mouth. She

Index

timing of, 52
release words, 68, 128
resources
    controlling, 17, 39
    group dynamics of, 15
    guarding, 209
retraining, 151–153
Reuck, Bill, 170
rewards
    for compliance, 105–108, 114, 139
    defined, 46
    for dominating behaviors, 18
    jackpots, 66
    negative reinforcement versus, 46–47
    stubborn as a mule dogs and, 142–144
    for stubbornness, 33
    training with, 65–66
Rottweilers
    bonding and, 135–136
    dominance of, 27
    guard-dog capabilities, 216
    predatory drive in, 220
    as reincarnated lawyers, 18–19
    response to leadership, 19
    sensitivity of, 34, 35
Rugaas, Turid, 170

S
Salukis
    high distractibility of, 33
    independence of, 30, 31
scenthounds, 33
Schutzhund Champion, 226–227
scruff shakes, 57
self-confidence, 160, 173
self-importance, 23–25, 129
self-rewarding behavior, 133, 134
sensitive dogs
    correcting, 165–166
    dominance and, 36
    nervous nellies as, 34–36
    stubbornness in, 149
    training challenges, 169–175
shaping process, 46, 77–79
Shelties, 38
Shiba Inu
    strong will of, 32, 105
    stubbornness of, 32, 32, 105, 140
shy dogs, 37–38, 156–165
sighthounds
    general characteristics, 33, 36
    high drive, 28
    as highly reactive, 23
    low impulse control, 37
    predatory drive aggression, 218, 220
    predatory drive in, 220
similar material, teaching separately, 51
sit command, 68–71, 226
sit-stay command, 88–91, 128, 231

social climbers, 14–15, 17
socializing
    guard dogs, 217, 227
    puppies, 43
    shy dogs, 38, 156–165
spaying dogs, 222
spray bottles, 201–202
stay command, 91
strong willed nature, 31–33
stubborn as a mule dogs
    independence, 30–31
    intermittent compliance, 149–153
    mule training, 4, 142
    retraining, 151–153
    strong willed nature, 31–33
    stubbornness, 4–5, 31–33, 105, 143
    training considerations, 143–149
submissive behaviors
    exposing bellies, 11
    training difficulties with, 14
    urinating, 11, 95, 195–196
submissive peeing, 11, 95, 195–196

T
temperament, training and, 37
Terriers. See also specific breeds
    biting behavior, 206
    high drive in, 28
    Picker (dog), 206
    predatory drive in, 220
    stubbornness in, 32
territory aggression, 214, 220, 221–223
territory marking, 10, 191–194
time-outs, 115, 116–118, 166
timing of reinforcement, 52
toxic foods, 65
toy ownership, 117
training issues
    for control freaks, 25–28, 30
    for nervous nellies, 33, 35–36, 38
    for sensitive dogs, 169–175
    for stubborn as a mule group, 31–33
training methods. See also power training
    calling down dogs, 222–223
    habit formation versus, 43–44
    mule training, 4, 142
    obedience training, 211–212
    philosophy about, 44–48
    with rewards, 65–66
    technical terms, 45–46
training precautions, 54–57
training rules, 49–53
training tools. See also leashes
    choke/slip collars, 5, 47, 62–64
    harnesses, 64, 83
    head halters, 83–85, 208, 222
    pinch/prong collars, 63
    treats, 63–65
treat blackmail

breaking, 99–101
defined, 99
Kelsey (dog), 99
treats, soliciting, 96–99
treat training
    controversy over, 47
    defined, 46
    effectiveness of, 45
    free feeding and, 66
    socializing dogs, 163–164
    as training tools, 63–65, 65
    varying treats, 66

U
Upping the Stakes technique
    compliance through bartering, 118–119
    compliance through insistence, 109–116
    compliance through missing out, 119
    compliance through reward, 105–108
    compliance through time-outs, 115, 116–118
    deterring barking, 201
    force versus enforce, 105
    overview, 104–105, 119–120
    playing hardball, 120–121
urinating
    greeting peeing, 196–197
    submissive peeing, 11, 95, 195–196

V
visual signals, unintended, 56
voice
    calming effect from, 168
    training rule for, 49, 112, 113

W
watch command
    bike chasing and, 107
    low impulse control and, 36
    overview, 76–81
    soliciting treats and, 97
West Highland White Terriers, 24
Whippets
    low impulse control of, 36
    predatory drive in, 220
wolf hybrids (wolf dogs), 11
wolf pack structure, 10–11
working breeds
    breed characteristics, 23–24, 26
    strong bonding, 134

Y
yawning, 171–172
yellow dogs, 157–158
"yes," 67–68, 71–72
Yorkshire Terriers, 220

Acknowledgements

Two trainers have and still do contribute to my base of knowledge about dog training. Since these two trainers are not credited directly in the text of this book I'd like to acknowledge Linda Bollinger and Tia Olson-Reinschmidt.

I'd also like to acknowledge Lois Storer, my mother. She put up with guinea pigs (a very large number of those), rats, mice, gerbils, hamsters, and a rescued tree squirrel; even though dear mother would quickly jump onto a chair should one of these escape. She also said to me when I was sixteen, "Peggy, that dog your older brother bought is always tied outside with nothing to do. Why don't you take him with you when you go to the horse stable." Brutus became one of the best dogs I ever owned.

About the Author

In her teens and early twenties, Peggy Swager started retraining problem horses. She also trained her own dogs—relying on techniques which were popular at the time, but that were often punishment based. When Peggy acquired a Jack Russell Terrier named Cookie, she never expected this dog to be so stubborn, high-drive, and strong willed. Cookie quickly taught Peggy that her old dog training techniques had to go.

Peggy expanded her lifelong studies in animal training to include dog training and behavior modification techniques. She became an instructor for puppy classes, basic obedience, and agility. As she honed her skills, not only did Peggy successfully reform Cookie's misbehaviors, she earned awards with Cookie in both agility and obedience. She has hosted clinics on dog training and given demonstrations on training techniques, and helps solve canine training issues with problem dogs.

In 2002, she won the Dog Writers of America award for best training article. Today, Peggy continues to write training articles for several magazines, including *Good Dog*, *Off Lead*, *Dog World*, *AKC Gazette*, *AKC Family Dog Magazine*, and *True Grit*. She is also the author of *The New Owner's Guide to Jack Russell Terriers*. She continues to help teach people to resolve issues with difficult-to-train dogs.